ART, MYTH, AND RITUAL

ART, MYTH, AND RITUAL

THE PATH TO POLITICAL

AUTHORITY IN ANCIENT CHINA

K. C. Chang

Harvard University Press

Cambridge, Massachusetts, and London, England

Library of Congress Cataloging in Publication Data

Chang, Kwang-chih.
    Art, myth, and ritual.
    Includes index.
    1. China–Civilization–To 221 B.C.   2. Political
science–China–History.   I. Title.
DS741.65.C53 1983   931   83-214
ISBN 0-674-04807-5 (cloth)
ISBN 0-674-04808-3 (paper)

ACKNOWLEDGMENTS

This book is based on selected course lectures given in 1981–82 at Harvard under its Core Curriculum. I would like to thank Emily Vermeule, chairman of the Subcommittee on Art and Literature for the Core, and Edward T. Wilcox, director of the General Education Program and the Core Program of Harvard College, for their encouragement to develop that course.

Chapter 4 was published in slightly different form as "The Animal in Shang and Chou Bronze Art," *Harvard Journal of Asiatic Studies* 41, (December 1981): 527–554.

For quotations from *Shu* and *Shih*, the two most important texts on ancient China, I have used the following translations by Bernhard Karlgren: *The Book of Documents* (Stockholm: Museum of Far Eastern Antiquities, 1950), and *The Book of Odes* (Stockholm: Museum of Far Eastern Antiquities, 1974). For the translation of *Ch'u Tz'u*, I have used David Hawkes, *Ch'u Tz'u: The Songs of the South* (Oxford: Clarendon Press, 1959). I am grateful to the Museum of Far Eastern Antiquities, to David Hawkes, and to Clarendon Press for permission to quote from these works. Unless otherwise noted, all other translations of Chinese texts are my own.

Many of the photographs used were supplied by Chinese colleagues; others were taken by me with the permission of the Chinese authorities. I extend thanks to all of my sources for their generosity and trust, and particularly to Higuchi Takayasu for his help in obtaining the photograph for the book's jacket.

In addition, I would like to thank Steve Burger for his help in photography, Nancy Lambert Brown for drawing the maps found in the front matter and in Figure 48, and Maria Kawecki for her careful and skillful editing. Special thanks are due Marjorie Balzer for bibliographic help on shamanism.

The sources of the figures are given at the end of the book. I thank the respective publishers for permission to reprint here those illustrations that appeared previously in other works.

CONTENTS

Contents

FIGURES

ART, MYTH, AND RITUAL

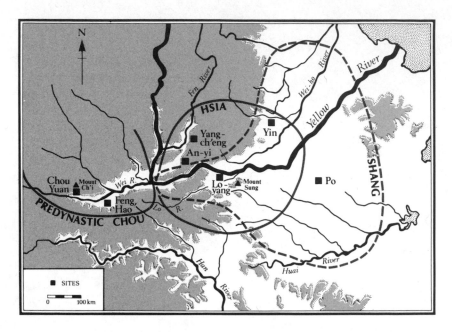

Map of ancient China, showing the approximate
areas of distribution of the three dynasties.

INTRODUCTION

Art and myth in ancient China were inextricably related to politics. We are quite accustomed to thinking of politics as a critical element in modern Chinese society. That it is equally so for ancient China is less commonly recognized, and my purpose here is to demonstrate this through a combination of data and insights derived not only from archaeology but also from literature and art.

The objective of the book is thus twofold. First, it provides a fundamental perspective for viewing the nature and structure of ancient Chinese civilization as having a strong political orientation. Second, it demonstrates that the study of ancient civilizations — at least the study of the ancient Chinese civilization — can be most rewarding if it deemphasizes traditional disciplinary barriers, a point I have made repeatedly in the past decade.[1]

The phrase "ancient China" refers to most of the two millennia before the Christian era, during which time the earliest historical civilization of China was created under the Three Dynasties — Hsia, Shang, and Chou.[2]

---

1. See K. C. Chang, *Inscribed Bronzes of the Shang and Chou: A Comprehensive Study* (in Chinese), Institute of History and Philology, Academia Sinica, Special Publication no. 62 (Taipei, 1973), p. i; idem, *Early Chinese Civilization* (Cambridge, Mass.: Harvard University Press, 1976), pp. v – xi.

2. Because of the rapid advances in the archaeology of ancient China, good, up-to-date texts on ancient China are unavailable. A classic in a Western language is Henri Maspéro, *China in Antiquity*, tr. F. A. Kierman (Amherst: University of Massachusetts Press, 1978). Another general text is Jacques Gernet, *Ancient China from the Beginnings to the Empire* (Berkeley: University of California Press, 1968). K. C. Chang, *The Archaeology of Ancient China* (New Haven: Yale University Press, 1977), focuses on the archaeological aspect only; and K. C. Chang, *Early Chinese Civilization* (Cambridge, Mass.: Harvard University Press, 1976), consists of a series of topical studies.

1

Traditional chronology places Hsia between 2205 and 1766 B.C., Shang between 1766 and 1122, and Chou between 1122 and 256. Except for the last date, all others are suspect, and specialists argue heatedly over them: no fewer than eighteen different dates have been proposed for the inception of the Chou dynasty.[3] For our purposes, these technical arguments are unimportant, because they are irresoluble. We will use round figures for the Three Dynasties: 2200–1750 for Hsia, 1750–1100 for Shang, and 1100–256 for Chou.

The ages preceding the Hsia dynasty — China's prehistory — can be reconstructed on the basis of two kinds of evidence. The first consists of myths and legends concerning the period before 2200, recorded in texts written during the Three Dynasties (actually for the most part during the latter half of the Chou dynasty). These pertain largely to the legends of ancient heroes and sages, which were systematized during the Han dynasty (206 B.C.–A.D. 220) into the San Huang (the "Three Sovereigns") and Wu Ti (the "Five Emperors"), illustrated in Figure 1. There are various versions of both sets, but the most common of the Three Sovereigns are Fu Hsi (the "First Man"), Sui Jen (or Chu Jung, the inventor of fire), and Shen Nung (the inventor of plant husbandry); and the Five Emperors are usually Huang Ti (the celebrated Yellow Emperor, the initiator of civilization), Chuan Hsü (the emperor in whose hands heaven was separated from earth), Ti K'u, Ti Yao, and Ti Shun.[4] Throughout most of Chinese history, these sages and heroes were accepted as historical personages, but in recent decades historians and folklorists have shown that most if not all of them were in fact ancient religious figures that had become "euhemerized" during the later Chou and the Han dynasties.[5]

The second kind of data on which one can reconstruct Chinese pre-

3. The eighteen dates are: 1122, 1116, 1111, 1076, 1075, 1070, 1067, 1066, 1057, 1050, 1049, 1047, 1045, 1030, 1029, 1027, 1025, and 1018. See K. C. Chang, "China," in *Chronologies in Old World Archaeology*, ed. Robert Ehrich, 3rd ed. (Chicago: University of Chicago Press, in press).

4. For some Western works on ancient Chinese mythology, see Henri Maspéro, "Légendes mythologiques dans le *Chou King*," *Journal Asiatique* 204 (January–March 1924): 1–100; Derk Bodde, "Myths of ancient China," in *Mythologies of the Ancient World*, ed. Samuel N. Kramer (New York: Doubleday, 1961), pp. 367–408; Sarah Allen, *The Heir and the Sage: Dynastic Legend in Early China* (San Francisco: Chinese Material Center, 1981).

5. The legendary history of ancient China began to be seriously questioned by empirically oriented historians during the 1920s, leading to the establishment of a "Doubting Antiquity School," which refused to recognize the historicity of Chinese history before the later part of the Shang dynasty. See Laurence A. Schneider, *Ku Chieh-kang and China's New History* (Berkeley: University of California Press, 1971).

1. Legendary figures of China (the San Huang
and Wu Ti) as depicted in a stone relief mural in
the funerary shrine of Wu Liang, in Chia-hsiang,
Shantung, carved in the mid-second century
A.D. The human figures in the middle register
represent the legendary heroes and sages as well
as the first and the last kings of the first (Hsia)
dynasty. From right to left: Fu Hsi and Nü Wa,
the world's parents, shown with their tails
intertwined; Chu Jung, creator of fire; Shen
Nung, inventor of agriculture, carrying his
digging stick; Huang Ti, initiator of civilization;
Chuan Hsü; Ti K'u; Ti Yao; Ti Shun; the Great
Yü, founder of the Hsia; and, the figure on the
far left, Chieh, the last Hsia king.

history is archaeological. Scientific archaeology of underground relics of ancient men and cultures was introduced into China from the West and from Japan in the beginning of the twentieth century.[6] The prehistoric account that has thus far been revealed by the excavations begins with man's early ancestors of almost two million years ago and continues on through the famous Peking Man of only about four hundred thousand years ago, the beginning of animal and plant husbandry of perhaps ten thousand years ago, and the growth of farming villages, until the very eve of the civilization of the Three Dynasties.[7] Possibly some of the prehistoric cultures were, in their later stages, created by some of the heroes and sages described in the traditional legends and myths, but prehistoric people left no texts in which their heroes were identified.

The Three Dynasties form the first period of Chinese history for which we have both texts and archaeological remains. This is not strictly true for the Hsia dynasty, since we have not yet discovered written records left by the Hsia themselves, whereas we do have such records from both the Shang and Chou.[8] But many later records pertaining to the Three Dynasties have been confirmed in essence by the Shang and Chou records, and the textual information on the Hsia may thus be considered much more reliable than anything that exists for the prehistoric (pre-Hsia) period. Such "later records" include, mainly, some of the so-called Confucian classics compiled during the latter half of the second millennium B.C.: *Yi, The Book of Changes; Shih, The Book of Odes; Shu, The Book of Documents; Ch'un Ch'iu, The Spring-and-Autumn Annals*, and its commentaries (*chuan*), especially those by Tso Ch'iu-ming, known as *Tso Chuan*; and *San Li*, or *The Three Books of Rituals*, including *Yi Li, Li Chi*, and *Chou Li*.[9] Useful information pertaining to the Three

6. For the introduction of scientific archaeology and its impact on Chinese historiography, see K. C. Chang, "Archaeology and Chinese historiography," *World Archaeology* 13 (October 1981): 156–169; and Li Chi, *Anyang* (Seattle: University of Washington Press, 1977).

7. For a recent synthesis of Chinese prehistory, see K. C. Chang, "In search of China's beginnings: New light on an old civilization, *American Scientist* 69 (March–April 1981): 148–160.

8. A very reliable survey of ancient Chinese literature is Burton Watson, *Early Chinese Literature* (New York: Columbia University Press, 1962). For special problems encountered in using these texts for historiographic research, see Cho-yun Hsu, *Ancient China in Transition* (Stanford: Stanford University Press, 1965), appendix entitled "Authenticity and dating of pre-Ch'in texts."

9. The most readily available translation of the Chinese classics into English is James Legge, *The Chinese Classics*, vols. 1–5 (Oxford: Clarendon Press 1872–1895); and idem, *The Li Ki*, vols. 27 and 28 of *The Sacred Books of the East*, ed. F. Max Müller (Oxford: Clarendon Press, 1885). Other translations are available, sometimes more up-to-date

Dynasties is also found in *Ch'u Tz'u,* or *The Elegies of Ch'u,* a collection of poetry by several Ch'u authors of central China of the late Chou period;[10] in philosophical works such as *Lun Yü* (The Confucian Analects)[11] and *Meng Tzu (Mencius)*;[12] and in several books, now in fragmentary form, unearthed in A.D. 280 from Chi prefecture in Honan, including *Chi Nien* (the so-called *Bamboo Annals*),[13] *Yi Chou Shu,* and *Mu T'ien Tzu Chuan.* These works are full of historical data but they are also full of myths, legends, and literary pieces, and they are essential to our understanding of the Chinese life in the Three Dynasties period.

Textual data on the Three Dynasties (many of them were recorded on bamboo or wooden slips and on silk and paper after the Three Dynasties and are known to have been subjected to corruption and distortion in the course of the ensuing two millennia) have been given strong support by recent discoveries of records from the Ch'in and Han dynasties, written on slips and silk (see Figure 2).[14] New kinds of data, both artifactual and inscriptional, have also been brought to light. In addition to numerous artifacts of stone, clay, wood, bamboo, silk, and bronze, which are indispensable for our examination into Bronze Age life, archaeology has also yielded inscriptional material of other kinds, principally inscriptions incised on oracle bones of the Shang and early Chou periods (Figure 3)[15] and those cast on ritual bronze vessels.[16]

---

and/or improved. For *Shih,* see Bernhard Karlgren, *The Book of Odes* (Stockholm: Museum of Far Eastern Antiquities, 1974); and Arthur Waley, *The Book of Songs* (New York: Grove Press, 1960). For *Yi,* see Richard Wilhelm and Cary F. Baynes, *The I Ching or Book of Changes* (Princeton: Princeton University Press, 1977). For *Shu,* see Bernhard Karlgren, *The Book of Documents* (Stockholm: Museum of Far Eastern Antiquities, 1950).

10. The definitive translation is David Hawkes, *Ch'u Tz'u: The Songs of the South* (Oxford: Clarendon Press, 1959).

11. Legge, *The Chinese Classics;* see also D. C. Lau, tr., *Confucius: The Analects* (Harmondsworth: Penguin Books, 1979).

12. Legge, *The Chinese Classics;* see also D. C. Lau, tr., (Harmondsworth: Penguin Books, 1970).

13. For a critical discussion of the usefulness of the *Bamboo Annals,* see David N. Keightley, "The *Bamboo Annals* and Shang-Chou chronology," *Harvard Journal of Asiatic Studies* 38 (December 1978): 423–438.

14. See Michael Loewe, "Manuscripts found recently in China: A preliminary survey," *T'oung Pao* 63 (1977): 99–136.

15. A detailed examination of the oracle bone inscriptions as historical data is David N. Keightley, *Sources of Shang History* (Berkeley: University of California Press, 1968).

16. Ancient bronze inscriptions have not received monographic treatment in a Western language, as far as I know. Both William Watson, *Ancient Chinese Bronzes* (Rutland, Vt.: Tuttle, 1962), and Li Xueqin, *The Wonder of Chinese Bronzes* (Peking: Foreign Languages Press, 1980), have substantial chapters devoted to the topic.

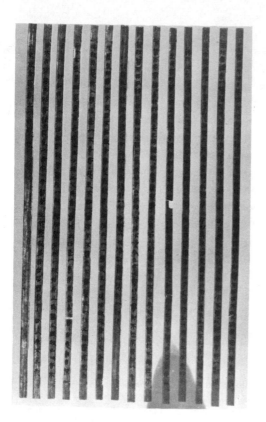

2. Inscribed bamboo slips of the Ch'in dynasty (left) and silk writing of the Han dynasty (right), recently excavated. Slips on left are about 28 centimeters long; fragment on right is about 18 centimeters long.

0   6 cm.

3. Inscribed oracle bone of the Shang dynasty,
excavated at Yin-hsü, in An-yang, Honan.

All these types of historical data are employed here to analyze the political culture of ancient China, and to seek an answer to a basic question: How did civilization and its concomitant, the political dynasties, arise in ancient China? The data lead to the conclusion that civilization evolved along with the dynasties because in China — as elsewhere — it was the manifestation of the accumulated wealth of a small segment of society, the dynasty. In our case we can demonstrate that this wealth was accumulated primarily through the exercise of political authority, and that the accrual of political authority in the Chinese context was facilitated by several interrelated factors: kinship hierarchy, moral authority of the ruler, military power, exclusive access to gods and to ancestors (as through rituals, art, and the use of writing), and access to wealth itself. By examining the history of these factors we can isolate some of the more convincing causes of the rise of political authority in ancient China. Insofar as the evolution of such authority is a universal theme, the Chinese case should be of more than provincial interest.

In this book the Three Dynasties are treated as a single unit, a unit also referred to as "ancient China." This is permissible, I believe, because the characteristics of the political culture in ancient China were in many important respects common throughout the period, and they even continued into the postancient period, however we define these periods. Profound changes in ancient Chinese society took place around 500–600 B.C., when the Iron Age began to replace the Bronze Age. Purists may wish to interpret the term "ancient China" in the title of this book as including only the period of the Three Dynasties up to the middle of the Spring-and-Autumn epoch. They will see, however, that much information from after that cutoff date has been woven here into the overall pattern of ancient art, myth, and politics, and that this pattern also applies to the later period.

1

CLANS, TOWNS,
AND THE POLITICAL
LANDSCAPE

Each of the Three Dynasties was founded by members of a different clan. Actually, in early China there were probably many hundreds of such clans, each characterized by a set of common features. Members of a clan traced their descent from the same mythological ancestor through the paternal line, although the actual fact of descent in the far remote past usually could not be genealogically demonstrated.[1] The myth of the ancestral birth gave rise in most cases to a name and an emblem ("totem") used by the entire clan.[2] Clan members supposedly all shared some

---

1. Some believe in the existence of an archaic society in Chinese history, in which descent was traced through the maternal line and in which women commanded higher political status than men. This belief is based on two very different sources. The first is the nineteenth-century evolutionist paradigm according to which every society goes through a matriarchal phase — a conviction that has been reinforced in Chinese historiography in the twentieth century by the adoption of Marxism as official doctrine. The second source consists of scattered textual accounts of a society in the remote past in which mothers were known (or recognized) while fathers were not. If there was indeed such a stage in Chinese history, it must have occurred long before the Three Dynasties. We know of no actual clans from the Three Dynasties period that were not patrilineal. For some earlier discussions by European sinologists on this issue, see A. Courady, *China* (Berlin: Pflugk-Harttung's Weltgeschichte, 1910), pp. 483ff; W. Koppers, "Die frage des Mutterrechts und des Totemismus im alten China," *Anthropos* 25 (September–December 1930): 981–1002; E. Erkes, "Der primat des Weibes im alten China," *Sinica* 10 (November 1935): 166–176; and W. Eberhard, *Localkulturen im alten China*, vol. 2 (Peking, 1942), pp. 96ff.

2. *Tso Chuan* entry for 715 B.C.: "When the Son of Heaven sends out a virtuous lord, he grants him [he ratifies] his clan name according to his birth." (Translations of Chinese texts are my own unless otherwise noted.)

special quality or character, and this was given as one of the reasons why they did not intermarry.[3]

Although we are certain that each of the many hundreds of these agnatic clans in ancient China had its own myth of ancestral origins, only a few have been preserved in the literature. These were myths of the clans whose members founded the major dynasties and other political houses.

The Hsia dynasty, the first political dynasty in traditional recorded history, was founded by members of the Ssu clan. Perhaps because of the greater antiquity of the dynasty, for which texts are as yet unknown, the mythical origin of the clan's ancestors is unclear. In one version[4] the mother of Yü, founder of the dynasty (Figure 4), gave birth to him as the result of eating some grains of Job's tears (*Coix lacryma-jobi*). (Job's tears were called *yi-ssu*, hence the name of the clan, and they are one of the oldest domesticated crops in Eastern Asia.) In another story, however, the clan's ancestor appears to have been born out of a rock. Yü's father, Kun, charged with the task of stemming a great flood, "stole from the [Supreme God] the 'swelling mold' (*hsi jang*) — a magical kind of soil which had the property of ever swelling in size. With this he tried to build dams which, through their swelling, would hold back the waters. When his efforts failed, the [Supreme God], angered by his theft, had him executed. There his body remained for three years [turning into a stone], until somebody . . . cut it open with a sword; thereupon Yü emerged from his father's belly."[5] This story is more or less repeated to account, as well, for the birth of Yü's son: "While digging a passage through a certain mountain, [Yü] was changed . . . into a bear. His wife, [the Lady of T'u Shan], seeing him, ran away and herself became changed to stone. She was pregnant at the time, and so when Yü pursued her and called out, 'Give me my son!' the stone split open on its north side and a son, Ch'i [which means 'to open'] came forth."[6] (See the appendix for lists of the kings of the Three Dynasties.)

3. *Kuo yü* (vol. 10, "Chin yü"): "People of the same clan name also have the same virtue, and people of the same virtue converge in mind, and people who converge in mind have the same goal. Persons of the opposite sexes but having the same goal do not marry, even if they may be very distant relations, for fear of committing incest."

4. *Lun Heng* ("Ch'i kuai p'ien"), by Wang Ch'ung (27–c. 97).

5. Derk Bodde, "Myths of Ancient China," in *Mythologies of the Ancient World*, Samuel N. Kramer (New York: Doubleday, 1961), p. 399.

6. Bodde, "Myths of Ancient China," p. 401.

4. The Great Yü as portrayed in the Wu Liang
Tz'u mural.

The Shang dynasty was founded by members of the Tzu clan, who were descendants of the clan's founder, Hsieh. According to Shang myth, an egg dropped by a dark bird was devoured by Hsieh's mother, who became pregnant as a result and later gave birth to him (Figure 5).[7] The myth of ancestral birth from a bird's egg was widespread in ancient times among the peoples in the eastern coastal areas of China and Northeast Asia,[8] a fact which seems to support the belief of many scholars that the Shang people had come from the east.

The last of the Three Dynasties, the Chou, was founded by members of the Chi clan, which derived its name — according to one account — from the name of a small river flowing in the clan's homeland. The clan's ancestor, Ch'i ("the Abandoned One") or Hou Chi ("Lord Millet"), shown in Figure 6, was according to the origin myth "Sheng min" (in *Shih*) a direct descendant of Supreme God himself, who made an imprint with his foot and caused Lady Yuan of the Chiang clan to become pregnant when she trod on the big toe of the footprint. "Sheng min" relates that after Chiang Yuan gave birth to Hou Chi, he was abandoned in a narrow lane, then in a far-off wood, and then on ice, but each time he was saved, by oxen and sheep, by woodcutters, or by birds. When he grew up, he became a specialist in plant husbandry, was adept in growing millet,

7. Poem "Hsuan niao," in *Shih*: "Heaven bade the dark bird / To come down and bear the Shang."

8. A longer version of a similar story relates the birth of Chu Meng, ancestor of the Fu-yü, a people on the northern coast of the Gulf of Chihli (Pohai Bay). As recorded in the "History of Kao-kou-li," in *Wei Shu* (written 551–554), the story is as follows: "Kao-kou-li was founded by the Fu-yü, who called their ancestor Chu Meng. Chu Meng's mother was a daughter of Ho-po (Lord of the Yellow River). Imprisoned in a room by the king of Fu-yü she was touched by the sun's rays. Whenever she moved away from the sunlight, it followed her. Soon she became pregnant and gave birth to an egg, which was so large that it could have held nearly five pints. The king gave the egg to the dogs, who refused to eat it. It was given to the pigs, who would not eat it either. It was then thrown out on the road, and cattle and horses walked away from it. It was thrown out into the wilderness, but the birds flew down to cover it with their feathers. The king of Fu-yü tried to cut it with a knife, but could not. He finally gave it back to its mother. The mother wrapped it and sheltered it in a warm place, and a baby boy broke the shell and emerged. After he grew up he was named Chu Meng."

5. The origin myth of the ancestor of the Shang. The bird is shown dropping an egg, and Chien Ti (right), who later devoured it, gave birth to Hsieh.

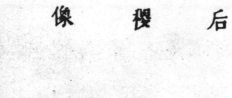

6. Portrait of the mythical figure Hou Chi,
ancestor of the Chou dynasty.

beans, and other plants, and began the practice of offering sacrifices.[9] In
another dynastic legend, "Mien," also in *Shih*, the origin of the human
race was compared to the spreading of young gourds. The ancestral birth
from bottle gourds is a common myth, and this could be another version
of the Chi clan origins.[10]

Since the Three Dynasties were founded by the three clans—Ssu, Tzu,
and Chi—the dynasties' rise and fall were in fact the rise and fall of the
fortunes of the individual clans in the political arena in which many clans
coexisted, and this fact—that political authority was wielded by social
groups basing their membership on blood relationships—is a prominent
feature of the ancient Chinese state. Furthermore, each of the clans was
itself highly stratified, again along blood lines. Each clan comprised a
number of lineage groups, and the members of each group were related
to one another according to a genealogically demonstrable relationship.
Individual lineages, and even individual members within each lineage,
possessed unequal degrees of political status.

9. See *Shih* ("Sheng Min"), as translated by Karlgren, in Bernhard Karlgren, *The Book of
Odes* (Stockholm: Museum of Far Eastern Antiquities, 1977).

> The one who first bore our tribe was (lady) Yuan of Chiang;

> . . . . .

> She trod on the big toe of God's footprint,
> She became elated, she was enriched, she was blessed,
> And so she became pregnant, and it came about quickly;
> She bore, she bred: that was Hou Chi.

> . . . . .

> They laid him in a narrow lane,
> The oxen and sheep between their legs nurtured him;
> They laid him in a forest on the plain,
> He was found by those who cut the forest of the plain;
> They laid him on cold ice,
> Birds covered and protected him;
> Then the birds went away, and Hou Chi wailed;
> It carried far, it was strong, his voice then became loud . . .

10. *Shih* ("Mien"), as translated by Karlgren, in part:

> Long drawn-out are the stems of the gourds
> When (our) people first was born,
> It came from Tu, from Tsu and Ch'i;
> The ancient prince T'an Fu, he moulded covers, he moulded caves;
> As yet they had no houses.

The lineage system of the Three Dynasties is not clearly understood, but the broad principle that political status was genealogically determined is not in question.[11] In a number of Chou texts we find clear explications of a system of lineage segmentation, resulting in the fission of the agnatic lineages and the establishment of the branch lineages in their own well-defined spatial domains. As a hypothetical example, consider a major lineage that might have ruled over an urban center with significant political authority. The lineage would have been one of a group of lineages all belonging to a certain clan, but let us assume that this lineage was superior to the others of the same clan and to the other clans within the territory of its rule. It could be termed the "royal" lineage — the ruler of its own dynasty. This lineage would be perpetuated by a line of male heirs, whose status would be determined by specified factors such as being the son of a primary wife or being the first-born among brothers.

At some point in the royal lineage's life there would arise reasons for sending one of its male members away from the royal domain to establish a new polity. He would be a brother, an uncle, or a cousin of the ruler, and he might be accompanied by a sizable group of people in order to relieve population pressure, to open up new arable land, or to shore up defense. Whatever the reason, he would be sent off with (a) his clan affiliation and emblem, (b) several groups of lineage members of one or more clans to provide both agricultural and industrial labor and military force, (c) title to the land of his newly established domain, (d) a new name for his new polity, and (e) ritual symbols and paraphernalia both to continue his ritual affiliation with his father's lineage and to manifest his new independence. In the new land he would build a new temple, in which his own tablet would eventually be placed as that of the founder of the new lineage. Thus, a new line of lineage segments would be initiated; they would be secondary lineages with respect to the stem lineage from which they had broken off, and their political as well as ritual status would likewise be secondary. This process of branching off would be repeated to form tertiary, quaternary, and subsequent levels of lineage segments. Such a system of segmentary lineages was thus also a system of decreasing political statuses.[12]

---

11. For a detailed discussion of the clan and lineage system of ancient China, see K. C. Chang, "The lineage system of the Shang and Chou Chinese and its political implications," in Chang, *Early Chinese Civilization* (Cambridge, Mass.: Harvard University Press, 1976), pp. 72–92.

12. The process of lineage fission and political enfeoffment lies at the core of the so-called

The focal points of the segmentary lineages were walled towns. The Chinese town, ancient as well as modern (Figure 7), was, in the words of Joseph Needham, "not a spontaneous accumulation of population, nor of capital or facilities of production, nor was it only or essentially a market-centre; it was above all a political nucleus, a node in the ad-

---

feng-chien system of the Chou dynasty, the words deriving from *feng*, "to put borders to [a piece of land]," and *chien*, "to establish [a ruler-ship over the land]." This term is often translated as "feudalism," but the application of the term does not imply that the Chinese system should be equated with the European institution. See Derk Bodde, "Feudalism in China," in *Feudalism in History*, ed. R. Coulborn (Hamden, Conn.: Archon Press, 1956).

The fundamental datum pertaining to the *feng-chien* system of early Chou is the following entry in *Tso Chuan*, under 505 B.C.: "When King Wu had subdued Shang, King Ch'eng completed the establishment of the new dynasty, and chose and appointed [the princes of] intelligent virtue, to act as bulwarks and screens to Chou. Hence it was that the duke of Chou gave his aid to the royal House for the adjustment of all the kingdom, he being most dear and closely related to Chou. To the duke of Lu there were given — a grand chariot, a grand flag with dragons on it, the *huang*-stone of the sovereigns of Hsia, and the [great bow], Fan-jo of Feng-fu. [The heads of] six clans of the people of Yin — the T'iao, the Hsü, the Hsiao, the So, the Ch'ang-shao, and the Wei-shao — were ordered to lead the chiefs of their kindred, to collect their branches, the remoter as well as the near, to conduct the multitude of their connexions, and repair with them to Chou, to receive the instructions and laws of the duke of Chou. They were then charged to perform duty in Lu, that thus the brilliant virtue of the duke of Chou might be made illustrious. Lands [also] were apportioned [to the duke of Lu] on an enlarged scale, with priests, superintendents of the ancestral temple, diviners, historiographers, all the appendages of State, the tablets of historical records, the various officers and the ordinary instruments of their offices. The people of Shang Yen were also attached; and a charge was given to Po Ch'in, and the old capital of Shao Kao was assigned as the center of his State.

"To K'ang Shu there were given a grand carriage, four flags — of various coloured silks, of red, of plain silk, and ornamented with feathered — and [the bell], Ta-lü, with seven clans of the people of Yin — the Tao, the Shih, the Fan, the Ch'i, the Fan, the Chi, and the Chung-k'uei. The boundaries of his territory extended from Wu-fu southwards to the north of P'u-t'ien. He received a portion of the territory of Yu-yen, that he might discharge his duty to the king, and a portion of the lands belonging to the eastern capital of Hsiang-t'u, that he might be able the better to attend at the king's journeys to the east. Tan Chi delivered to him the land, and Mao Shu the people. The charge was given to him, as contained in the 'Announcement to K'ang,' and the old capital of Yin was assigned as the center of his State. Both in Wei and Lu they were to commence their government according to the principles of Shang, but their boundaries were defined according to the rules of Chou.

"To T'ang Shu there were given a grand carriage, the drum of Mi-hsü, the *Chüeh kung* mail, the bell *Ku-hsien*, nine clans of the surname Huai, and five presidents over the different departments of office. The charge was given to him, as contained in the 'Announcement of T'ang,' and the old capital of Hsia was assigned as the center of his State. He was to commence his government according to the principles of Hsia, but his boundaries were defined by the rules of the Jung." Translated by James Legge, *The Chinese Classics*, vol. 5 (Oxford: Clarendon Press, 1872), p. 754.

ministrative network, and the seat of the bureaucrat [or] . . . the ancient feudal lord."[13] The construction of the town was, in fact, in its impetus, a political act that gave the new lineage its new seat of power, typically in a new land. In *Shih* we read a description of one such political act, involving the founding of a royal capital by a predynastic ancestor of the Chou people:

The ancient prince T'an-fu,
At daybreak he galloped his horses;
He followed the bank of the Western river,
He came to the foot of (mount) Ch'i;
And so together with the lady Chiang
He came and lingered (there) and took up an abode.

The plain of Chou was rich and ample;
Even the *chin* and *t'u* plants [bitter herbs] were sweet like honey-cakes;
And so he started, he planned,
He notched our tortoises [for divination];
And so he stopped; he halted, he built houses here.

And so he remained quiet, he stopped;
He went to the left, he went to the right,
He made boundaries, he made division,
He measured to the cubit, he laid out acres;
From west he went east,
Everywhere he took the task in hand.

And so he called the Master of Works,
He called the Master of Multitudes,
He made them build houses;
Their plumb-lines were straight;
They lashed the boards and thus erected the building frames;
They made the temple in careful order.

In long rows they collected it,
In great crowds they measured it out,
They pounded it, (the walls) rising high;
They scraped and went over them again, (so they became) solid;
A hundred tu [of walls] all rose;
The drums could not keep pace!

13. Joseph Needham, et al., *Science and Civilization in China*, vol. 4, pt. 3, "Civil Engineering and Nautics," (Cambridge: Cambridge University Press, 1971), p. 71.

7. A modern Chinese walled town, Wang-yeh-fu, in Ninghsia, 1923.

And so he raised the outer space;
The outer gate was high;
He raised the principal gate;
The principal gate was grand;
He raised the grand Earth-altar,
From which the great armies marched![14]

The poem describes virtually everything about an ancient Chinese town that is significant: it was built on a piece of largely vacant land, according to a plan (Figure 8); it consisted of a pounded earthen wall with important buildings inside (Figure 9); and it served as the political seat of the lord (in this case a Chou ruler from the Chi clan), who were the founders of a new lineage line. Furthermore, the very town whose construction is so vividly narrated in this ancient poem is even now being excavated under Mount Ch'i in central Shensi, after having lain buried for more than three thousand years (Figures 10, 11).[15]

Thousands of such towns dotted the North China landscape, and the sites of many have been discovered in recent decades, from all three dynasties. Actually, the archaeological manifestation of the Hsia dynasty is still a controversial issue, but an increasing number of scholars identify the so called Erh-li-t'ou Culture with the Hsia.[16] In traditional texts the Hsia dynasty is located in southwestern Shansi and northwestern Honan, with Mount Sung in central Honan as its sacred mountain.[17] The sites of the Erh-li-t'ou Culture — discovered by archaeologists only since the 1950s — are found in this area, and their available radiocarbon dates suggest late third and early second millennium B.C., the traditional temporal span of Hsia. The best excavated of the Erh-li-t'ou sites include those

14. *Shih* ("Mien") in Bernhard Karlgren, *The Book of Odes* (Stockholm: Museum of Far Eastern Antiquities, 1974), pp. 189–190.

15. K. C. Chang, *The Archaeology of Ancient China* (New Haven: Yale University Press, 1977; rpt. 1981). The appendix entitled "Highlights of Chinese Archaeology, 1976–80" has a brief description of the contemporary archaeology in the Plain of Chou.

16. See K. C. Chang, "The origin of Shang and the problem of Xia in Chinese archaeology," in *The Great Bronze Age of China: A Symposium*, George Kuwayama, ed. (Los Angeles: Los Angeles Museum of Art, 1983), pp. 10–15.

17. The best summary of traditional texts on Hsia geography is Yen Keng-wang, "Hsia capital locations and the Erh-li-t'ou culture" (in Chinese), *The Mainland Magazine* (*Ta-lu Tsa-chih*), 61 (May 1980): 1–17.

8. This Han dynasty tile with its "Four Deities" picture gives a microcosmic symbolization of an ancient Chinese town with its square shape and cardinal orientation. The four directional animals are a black turtle-snake on the north (bottom); a red bird on the south (top); a green dragon on the east (left); and a white tiger on the west (right).

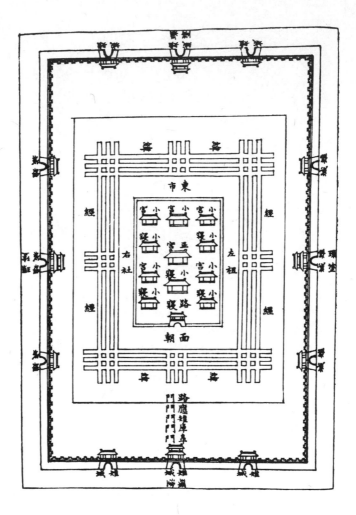

9. Idealized plan of the Chou dynasty royal
capital (Lo-yang); with rectangular city wall,
three gates on each side, nine major avenues east-
west and nine north-south, royal palaces at the
center, markets in the north, the ancestral temple
east of the palace, the earth altar west of the
palace, and the Hall of Audience south of the
palace. All buildings had their main doorways
open to the south.

10. Recent excavations in the Plain of Chou, described in "Mien" in the *Book of Odes.* Top: The Plain of Chou under Mount Ch'i. Bottom: Exposed floors of a predynastic house complex.

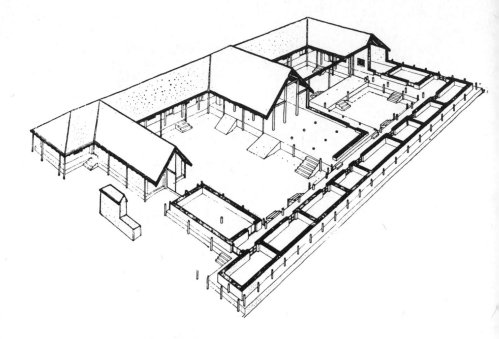

11. Reconstruction of some of the recently excavated predynastic and early dynastic houses of the Chou in the Plain of Chou, Shensi.

at Tung-hsia-feng in Hsia prefecture in Shansi and at Wang-ch'eng-kang in Teng-feng, Honan.[18] Both are sites enclosed by walls of pounded earth. According to one legendary account (*Shih pen*, "Tso pien"), Kun, the aforementioned father of Yü, the Hsia dynasty's founder, was the culture hero credited with the first building of walled towns.

Archaeological sites of the Shang dynasty number in the dozens, but in the oracle bone inscriptions of the Shang dynasty at Yin-hsü (near An-yang, the ruins of Yin, the last dynastic capital) about a thousand town names are mentioned.[19] These towns are concentrated in the area to the east of Hsia, incorporating the modern provinces of western Shantung, southern Hopei, eastern Honan, and northern Anhwei and Kiangsu (Figure 12). Early Chou dynasty sites, on the other hand, are located in the western part of North China, largely in the east-central portion of Shensi—namely, the middle and lower Wei river valley.[20] At some of these Shang and Chou sites are found remains of pounded earth walls, but at other sites no such walls have yet come to light. The absence of walls could be archaeologically accidental; many of the sites have not been investigated thoroughly, and many of the walls could have been largely obliterated by erosion and disturbance. But the towns were in any event more important than their walls; walls may have been unnecessary where defense needs did not exist, or they could have been built with timber. The planning and the political function of the towns were the same with or without earthen walls. The thousands of towns that dotted the Three Dynasties' political landscape were linked together—by invisible lines, as it were—into hierarchical systems of administrative control and wealth distribution, and the town hierarchies largely coincided with the hierarchies of clans and lineages. Each "state," or *kuo*, in ancient China was thus a network of towns linked in various hierarchical levels. At the beginning of the Three Dynasties, there were numerous such states, each probably consisting of a smaller number of towns. As time progressed the number of states decreased, but the number of towns within each state increased, through a process of continual subjugation. According to Ku Tsu-yü (1624–1680), there were ten

18. A brief discussion of the two sites in light of Hsia history is found in Chou Yung-chen, "The search for the Hsia culture," *China Reconstructs* 27 (November 1978), pp. 48–50.

19. K. C. Chang, *Shang Civilization* (New Haven: Yale University Press, 1980), p. 210.

20. For the geographic distribution of Shang and Chou sites, see K. C. Chang, "Sandai archaeology and the formation of states in ancient China: Processual aspects of the origins of Chinese civilization," in *The Origin of Chinese Civilization*, ed. David N. Keightley (Berkeley: University of California Press, 1983), pp. 495-521.

12. Sections of the Shang dynasty city wall in Cheng-chou, Honan. Height of remaining sections is about 2.5 meters.

thousand *kuo* at the time of the Great Yü. By the time of T'ang, the founder of the Shang dynasty, the number of *kuo* had dropped to more than three thousand. At the time of King Wu Wang of Chou, conqueror of the Shang dynasty, only eighteen hundred *kuo* remained. At the beginning of the Eastern Chou (771 B.C.), twelve hundred *kuo* were left, and at the end of the Spring-and-Autumn period (481 B.C.) that number decreased to just over a hundred, of which only fourteen were considered major states.[21]

The interactions among the various town hierarchies included such activities as political alliance, trade, war, and marriage. Shifting political alliances reduced the number of political units from the total number of individual towns to a number of *kuo*, and in each of the Three Dynasties one of the states appeared to command preeminent status. The states of Hsia, Shang, and Chou, however, were merely the most prominent during their respective dynasties; they were by no means the only states that existed.

A few comments on marriage practices will serve to elaborate our discussion of lineage hierarchies.

The first recorded marriages between states concern the predynastic Chou kings Wang Chi and Wen Wang. Wang Chi's wife came from Shang, as related in the poem "Ta ming" in *Shih*:

> The lady Chung Jen of Chi came from the Yin-Shang,
> She came and married in Chou;
> She became bride in the capital;
> And so together with (her husband) Wang Chi she practised the virtue;
> T'ai Jen became pregnant and bore this Wen Wang.[22]

Moreover, one of Wen Wang's consorts may also have come from Shang. The same ode quoted above contains the following passage:

---

21. Ku Tsu-yü (1624–1680), *Tu Shih Fang-yü Chi-yao* (Significant notes on geography in the reading of history), vol. 1.

22. Karlgren, *The Book of Odes*, p. 188. The same marriage is described in another ode, "Ssu-chai" (ibid., p. 192):

> Reverent was T'ai Jen,
> The mother of Wen Wang;
> Beloved was lady Chiang of Chou,
> The wife in the (royal) house in the capital.

Heaven looked down upon the world below,
And its appointment lighted on (him) —
When Wen Wang started his action,
Heaven made for him a mate,
To the north of the Hsia (river),
On the banks of the Wei (river);
Wen Wang was fine;
And in a great state there was the young lady.
In a great state there was the young lady,
She looked as if she were a younger sister of Heaven;
Wen fixed on a lucky day,
And went in person to meet her on the Wei (river);
He arranged boats to form a bridge;
Amply illustrious was the splendour.
The appointment came from Heaven;
It gave the apointment to this Wen Wang,
In Chou, in the capital;
The lady-successor was (a girl from) Hsin;
The eldest daughter (of Hsin) performed her functions,
And she staunchly bore Wu Wang;
(Heaven said:) "I shall protect and help you and appoint you,
To march and attack the great Shang."[23]

Although the poem does not explicitly name Shang as the state of origin of Wen Wang's bride, the allusion to "a great state" has led scholars to suspect that the lady did indeed come from Shang; in fact, in reliable texts, Hsin is referred to as the dominion of a Shang lord.[24] Ku Chieh-kang has long cited a reference in *Yi* (*The Book of Changes*) — "Ti Yi gives his daughter in marriage"[25] — as relating to the same story, namely, the marriage of Ti Yi's daughter to Wen Wang of Chou. If this is true, it appears that at the time of this marriage the political status of the wife-giver (Shang) was higher than that of the wife-receiver (Chou), a situation consistent with relative statuses in political marriages found in some ethnographic records.[26]

The situation was, however, somewhat different in the late Chou period, for which we have better records and more detailed data pertaining to interstate marriages. In ancient China, bilateral cross-cousin

23. Karlgren, *The Book of Odes*, p. 188.

24. Hsin, in fact, was the small state from whch Yi Yin, T'ang's prime minister, came.

25. Ku Chieh-kang, "Stories in the texts of the *Book of Changes*" (in Chinese), *Yenching Journal of Chinese Studies* 6 (December 1929): 979.

26. E. R. Leach, "Structural implications of matrilateral cross-cousin marriage," in Leach, *Rethinking Anthropology* (London: London School of Economics, 1961; orig. pub. 1951).

marriages were probably permitted — that is, a man could marry his father's sister's daughter or his mother's brother's daughter. The most important evidence for this is in kinship terminology found in Chou texts:[27]

chiu: mother's brother; husband's father; wife's father
ku: father's sister; husband's mother
sheng: sister's son; father's sister's son; mothers brother's son; wife's brother; sister's husband; daughter's husband.

Bilateral cross-cousin marriage is known to be a rather flexible institution, and it has a wide enough range for specific adjustments under particular circumstances. That this custom was probably practiced in ancient China has been noted by several scholars.[28] Within the framework of the bilateral cross-cousin marriage, strong emphases were sometimes placed exclusively on either the patrilateral (marrying father's sister's daughter only) or the matrilateral (marrying mother's brother's daughter only) variety under certain circumstances. And the guiding principle for the shifting emphases appears to be the political status of the intermarrying parties. Patrilateral cross-cousin marriage tended to take place among political equals, whereas matrilateral cross-cousin marriage tended to take place as a contributing factor in the delicate and dynamic balance of political power between lineages of unequal status. It has been suggested that some of the endogamous marriages within the Shang royal house were patrilateral cross-cousin marriages,[29] but the evidence for this is controversial and there is no other known occurrence in ancient China outside that context.

On the other hand, several interesting facts in Eastern Chou texts strongly point to the practice of matrilateral cross-cousin marriage.

1. In *Tso Chuan* intermarrying states referred to each other as "maternal uncle and sororal nephew states," and this designation strongly suggests the probability that the relationship between the intermarrying states was an ongoing one.

27. The most authoritative writings on ancient Chinese kinship terminology are those of Ruey Yin-fu; see his *Collected Works* (*China: The Nation and Some Aspects of Its Culture*) (in Chinese), sect. G, "The Chinese family system," and sect. H, "The Chinese kinship system," (Taipei: Yee Wen, 1972), pp. 723–1028.

28. Ruey, *Collected Works,* pp. 723–1028; Marcel Granet, *Chinese Civilization* (London: Paul, Trench, Trübner, 1930), p. 157.

29. See K. C. Chang, "*T'ien kan*: A key to the history of the Shang," in *Studies in Early Civilization,* ed. David Roy and T. H. Tsien (Hong Kong: Chinese University of Hong Kong Press, 1978), pp. 13–42.

2. Such an ongoing relationship is referred to in *Tso Chuan* in terms that do not necessarily apply to the actual relationship between any two particular rulers, but that apply to the two states *as states*, regardless of generation. Under the Twelfth Year entry of Duke Chao (528 B.C.), for example, the state of Ch'i is referred to as the "king's maternal uncle," even though there were cases where Ch'i rulers married daughters of Chou's rulers.

3. According to marriage records that I have found in *Tso Chuan*, there was a distinct tendency for the marriages between different lineages of different clans to be one-way rather than reciprocal. Figure 13 shows some of the marriage relations between the two most powerful eastern states: Lu, of Chi clan, and Ch'i, of Chiang clan. The dukes of Lu, a brother state of Chou, married women of Ch'i lineage of the Chiang clan, among others; they rarely gave their sisters and daughters in marriage to Ch'i rulers, but frequently married them off to men of other states. The Ch'i dukes, on the other hand, married their daughters to men of Lu but obtained their women mainly from other states. Even though it can be said that the Ch'i (of Chiang clan) married their women into the Chi clan, and also sometimes married women from the Chi clan, it is important to note that the specific lineages into which their daughters married and from which their wives came were different, even though these different lineages were all of the Chi clan. Taking the lineage rather than the clan for comparison, we see clearly that more women were exchanged one way than the other.

4. In the available records we often see a difference in political status between the maternal uncle and sororal nephew states, and that the wife-receivers seem to enjoy a higher political and/or ritual status than the wife-givers.[30] It is particularly interesting to note in this connection that when a king married his daughter to one of his lords he would ask a lord from a brother state to "give the bride away." In a commentary to *Tso Chuan*, Tu Yü explains that this was because of the "inequity of ranks." In other words, although a king's daughter had to be married to someone whose lineage could not possibly be politically superior to the king's, a compromise was made so that the king's lineage would not suffer loss of dignity by an inferior alliance.

30. Francis L. K. Hsu, "Observations on cross-cousin marriage in China," *American Anthropologist* 47 (January–March 1945): 83–103.

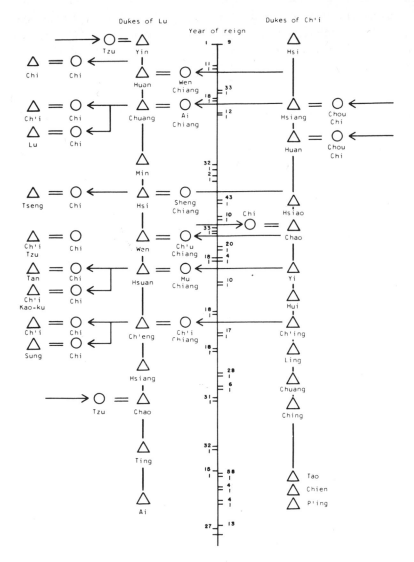

13. Marriage relations between some Lu and Ch'i dukes, 722–468 B.C., according to *Tso Chuan*.

In sum, available evidence from the Three Dynasties makes it clear that the political landscape of ancient China was dotted with hundreds of thousands of towns inhabited by members of discrete clans and lineages, and that these towns were linked in political hierarchies according to the kinship relations and interaction patterns of their inhabitants.

2

MORAL AUTHORITY AND COERCIVE POWER

The hierarchy of towns and of clans and lineages outlined in the previous chapter gives an idealized portrait of the power structure, a system that probably worked most of the time but whose balance was delicate at best. Clans, each claiming divine descent, competed for a rulership for which most if not all of them qualified in the mythological sense; within the clans the lineages, after many degrees of ramification, became scattered and their status claims became fine and relative and less than clear-cut. In other words, the kinship system by itself could not maintain the status hierarchy indefinitely. Other factors had to enter the balance sheet.

One of the more lofty of these factors affecting the political balance among the multitude of contenders was an evaluation of worth based on earned points of merit. It was not enough to be born to rule; one had to have earned the right to rule by deeds deserving the support of the ruled. The poem "Huang yi" describes why the Chou dynasty was the chosen ruler, and not the Hsia or the Shang:

> August is God on High;
> Looking down, he is majestic;
> He inspected and regarded the (states of) the four quarters,
> He sought tranquility for the people.
> These two kingdoms [Hsia and Shang],
> Their government had failed;
> Throughout those states of the four (quarters)
> He investigated and estimated;
> God on High brought it to a settlement;
> Hating their extravagance,

33

He looked about and turned his gaze to the West;
And here he gave an abode [among the Chou].[1]

This judgment on the part of God, based on the success or failure of the governments and on the rulers' extravagance or temperance, was called "heaven's mandate." This term, *t'ien ming*, attributing the choice to "heaven," represents a Chou concept.[2] It is doubtful that the Hsia and Shang used the same term. But the idea of rulership based on "deservedness" — whether from the point of view of God or from the point of view of the governed — goes back at least to the Shang. The Hsia, of course, did not seize the dominant rulership from a previous dynasty and did not need any moral justification for thier own supreme status. The Shang, however, did seize power from the Hsia and gave ample justification for their actions. *Shu* contains a document purporting to be a speech given by T'ang, the dynasty's founder, to his people on their way to vanquish the Hsia dynasty, under its last monarch, Chieh:

> The king said: Come, you multitudes, all listen to my words. It is not that I, the small child, dare act so as to start rebellion. The lord of Hsia has much guilt; Heaven has charged (me) to kill him. Now, you multitude there, you say: Our ruler (king Chieh) has no compassionate care for our multitude, he sets aside our husbandry works and has an injurious government. I have heard the words of you all; the lord of Hsia has guilt, I fear God on High, I dare not but punish him. Now you will surely say that Hsia's guilt is such as I say. The Hsia king in all (ways) obstructs the efforts of the multitude, in all (ways) he injures the city of Hsia, the multitude are all slack and disaffected. They say: That one [Chieh] daily injures and destroys, I and you shall all together perish. Such is the conduct of (the king) of Hsia. Now I will necessarily march. — May you support me, the One Man, to apply Heaven's punishment. I will then greatly reward you. May there be none of you who do not believe me. I do not eat my words. If you do not obey the words of this proclamation, I will kill you and your wife and children; there will be nobody who will be pardoned.[3]

Chieh's fate was, of course, eventually also the fate of Chòu, the last monarch of the Shang dynasty, who was in turn vanquished by the Chou people when he incurred hatred for his despotic actions. Mencius lumped

1. In Bernhard Karlgren, *The Book of Odes* (Stockholm: Museum of Far Eastern Antiquities, 1974), p. 194.

2. The Chou idea of the "mandate of heaven" is well discussed in Fu Ssu-nien, *Hsing Ming Ku Hsün Pien-cheng* (A critical analysis of the archaic meanings of the concepts *hsing* and *ming* (in Chinese) (Li-Chuang: Institute of History and Philology, Academia Sinica, 1940); and in Kuo Mo-jo, *Ch'ing-t'ung Shih-tai* (The Bronze Age) (in Chinese) (Chungking: Wenchih, 1945). For a discussion in English, see Donald J. Munro, *The Concept of Man in Early China*, (Stanford: Stanford University Press, 1969), pp. 84–90; and K. C. Chang, *Early Chinese Civilization* (Cambridge, Mass.: Harvard University Press, 1976), pp. 191–192.

3. Translation from Karlgren, *The Book of Documents*, p. 20.

Chieh and Chòu together as "mutilators, cripplers, and outcasts"; killing these kings, in his opinion, was just punishment and was by no means regicide.[4]

Thus, political dynasties fell because the king misbehaved and no longer deserved to rule. On the other hand, the founder of the new dynasty accomplished his meritorious deed by overthrowing the old, an action that was taken in response to the call of the multitude. The dynastic cycle of ancient China, then, has nothing to do with the rise and fall of the civilization; it merely signifies the shifting political fortunes of specific social groups whose rulers gain or lose their claim to the moral authority to rule.

Obviously the idea that a king's claim to rule was founded on merit may be characterized as a Confucian ideal,[5] but it was actually appealed to by both the Shang and the Chou as justification for their rule and must be regarded as a part of the art of governance in ancient China. A reading of the documents in *Shu* supports this point. Besides, as the above-quoted *Shu* document makes quite clear, the moral authority of the new dynasty was only one side of the coin. On the other side was a threat: "If you do not obey me, I will kill you and your wife and children; no one will be pardoned." What were some of the major sources of coercive power that enabled ruling groups to carry out such threats?

The lineage (*tsu*) itself was probably the most important social framework for coercion; *tsu* rules were the society's fundamental law. "The oracle bone character for *tsu* has two elements, a flag above and an arrow below [Figure 14]. Ting Shan's interpretation, that it originally signified a military unit, is generally accepted. In ancient China the association of flags with military units is well known, and in oracle bone inscriptions *tsu* are shown to be action units in military campaigns. Its size was probably a hundred strong on an average, the hundred adult men coming from a hundred households."[6] Thus, the leader of a *tsu* was not only the head of a lineage or sublineage but also a military commander, and his orders in civic as well as military affairs were to be obeyed. Defiance of a *tsu* leader could be punished severely, by mutilation or even death. The word for king, *wang*, the supreme head of all lineages, derives according to one hypothesis from the pictograph of an

---

4. Translation from D. C. Lau, *Mencius* (Harmondsworth: Penguin, 1970), bk. 1, pt. B.

5. Donald J. Munro, in *The Concept of Man in Early China*, calls the moral pretensions the Confucian "path to privilege."

6. K. C. Chang, *Shang Civilization* (New Haven: Yale University Press, 1980), p. 163.

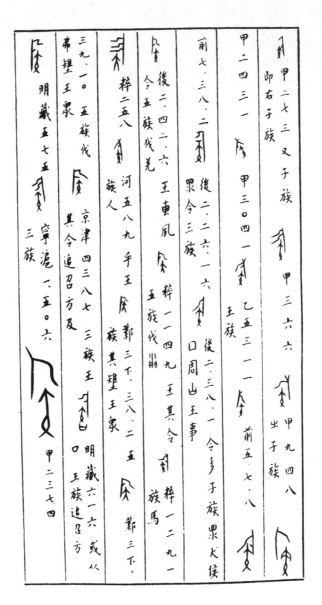

14. The character *tsu*, as seen in Shang dynasty
oracle bone inscriptions. The character is
illustrated here in several sizes and with slight
variations.

executioner's ax (Figure 15).[7] In Bronze Age China one of the main uses for bronze was in the making of weaponry, including pivotal parts of the fearsome horse-drawn chariot (Figure 16).

During the Three Dynasties, rules of behavior within the *tsu* were codified in rituals, which, most Chinese legal historians agree, were in fact laws.[8] The power of the lineage lords over their subjects was manifested in the ritual obligations of lineage members. Members of the same patrilineage traced their common descent to acknowledged male ancestors, a fact that was symbolized by and crystallized in the ancestor cult. *Yi Li* gives us an account of the procedures and details of some of the related rites, but we are best acquainted with some of the tangible aspects of these cults. First, there was the ancestral temple, which not only provided the setting for the rituals but was also a symbol in itself, as the center of rituals and of state affairs. The several levels of temples[9] probably coincided with the levels of lineage subdivision (Figure 17). It is implied in *Tso Chuan* (Twelfth Year of Duke Hsiang, 562 B.C.) that there were three levels of kin groups: *hsing, tsung,* and *tsu.* There were also three levels of ancestral temples: *tsung, tsu,* and *mi.* Each of these groups had, above all, an ancestral temple at the corresponding level as the center of its kinship cosmos. In *Li Chi* ("Ch'ü li"), we read: "When a superior man (high in rank) is about to engage in building, the ancestral [*tsung*] temple should have his first attention, the stables and arsenal the next, and the residences the last. In all preparations of things by (the head of) a [family], the vessels of sacrifice should have the first place; the victims supplied from his revenue, the next; and the vessels for use at meals, the last."[10] The importance of the ancestral temples and their para-

---

7. Lin Yün, "Shuo wang" (A discourse on *wang*) (in Chinese), *K'ao-ku* 1965 (6): 311–312.

8. See Mei Chung-hsieh, "Law and ritual" (in Chinese), in *Chung-kuo Fa-chih Shih Lun Chi* (Studies of Chinese legal history), ed. Hsieh Kuan-sheng and Cha Liang-chien (Taipei: Institute of Law, Chinese Culture College, 1968), pp. 137–145; and several other essays in the same collection. In the ancient Chinese classics, the relationship between *fa* (law) or *hsing* (punishment) and *li* (rituals) has always been clearly stated. An example is *Ta Tai Li Chi* ("Li ch'a"): "*Li*, ritual, is to prohibit something from happening, and *fa*, law, is to prohibit it after it has happened." Confucius himself stated: "Guide them by edicts, keep them in line with punishments, and the common people will stay out of trouble but will have no sense of shame. Guide them by virtue, keep them in line with the rites, and they will, besides having a sense of shame, reform themselves." D. C. Lau, tr., *Confucius: The Analects* (Harmondsworth: Penguin, 1979), p. 63.

9. Ling Shun-sheng, "Chung-kuo tsu-miao chih ch'i-yuan" (The origin of ancestral temples in China), *Bulletin of the Institute of Ethnology, Academia Sinica* 7 (Spring 1959): 141–184.

10. Translated by James Legge, *Li Ki*, in *The Sacred Books of the East*, vol. 27 (Oxford: Clarendon Press, 1885), p. 105.

15. Two bronze executioner's axes of the Shang dynasty. The left one (about 32 centimeters tall) was excavated from Su-fu-t'un, Yi-tu, Shantung, from an area probably occupied by another state contemporary with Shang. The one on the right (about 40 centimeters tall) was excavated from Yin-hsü, An-yang, Honan.

16. Remains of a Shang dynasty horse chariot
found recently at Yin-hsü.

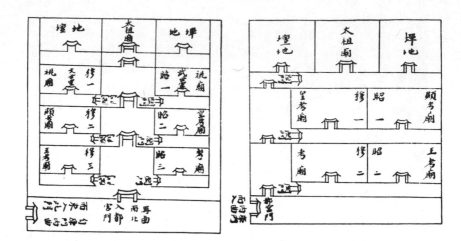

17. Two levels of ancestral temples. Temples on the left were those of Chou dynasty kings, with the temple of the founder at the center and three temples of the remote ancestors on each side. Temples on the right were those of a feudal lord, with only two temples on each side.

phernalia reflects the importance of ancestral rituals in the Chou institution. *Li Chi* ("Chi t'ung") makes this clear:

> Of all the methods for the good ordering of men there is none more urgent than the use of *li*. *Li* are of five kinds, and there is none of them more important than . . . *chi* [rituals].
>
> [Rituals] . . . are not a thing coming to a man from without; it issues from within him, and has its birth in his heart. When the heart is deeply moved, expression is given to it by ceremonies; and hence, only men of ability and virtues can give complete exhibition to the idea of [rituals].[11]

To reinforce such rules that were supposed to "issue from within," authorities made periodic inspections among the lords to see whether ancestral rites were properly performed. According to *Li Chi* ("Wang chih"), if the king found that ancestral rites were not being correctly observed, the lords were to be degraded. To vanquish a state and a system of government, an enemy state could assure destruction by breaking up the ancestral temples and looting the symbolic treasures.[12]

If the rituals and their tangible associations such as temples, tablets, and treasures provided the sanction, the reminder, and the symbol for the solidarity of the lineages, then myths provided the charter, giving the *raison d'être* for such groups. Almost invariably, according to the hero myths, the lineage ancestors had performed meritorious deeds, and it was precisely for their merits and deeds that ancestors were honored in the rites. *Kuo Yü* ("Lu yü") and *Li Chi* ("Chi fa") both specify the same criteria that were needed in order for an ancestor to merit a place in the ritual calendar: "According to the institutes of the sage kings about sacrifices, sacrifice should be offered to him who had given (good) laws to the people; to him who had laboured to the death in the discharge of his duties; to him who had boldly and successfully met great calamities; and to him who had warded off great evils . . . Only men and things of this character were admitted into the sacrificial canon."[13] This is to say that ancestors earned their places by merit and not merely by birth, a point discussed earlier. Myths are an integral part of the ritual system of the ancestor cult in the Shang and Chou periods, and "it was in their [the grandee houses'] interest to keep alive every scrap of tradition that showed their forefathers as powerful sages and good lords, and their opponents and foes as rebels and miscreants, doomed to failure and to loss

11. Legge, *Li Ki*, p. 236.
12. *Tso chuan*, entries under 552 B.C. and 606 B.C.
13. *Li Ki*, pp. 26–28.

of sacrificing descendants."[14] It is in this spirit, presumbly, that in *Li Chi* ("Chi t'ung") we find the following statement: "For the progeny who maintain the ancestral temple and the state, it is deceitful to enumerate the deeds of ancestors if they did not exist; imbecile not to know the deeds if they existed; unkind not to publicize the deeds if they were known." Dynastic rulers reaped the largest rewards by publicizing their deeds, of course, but rulers at all levels acquired their status by earning it also. Clan ancestors were by necessity culture heroes. The Great Yü, founder of the Ssu clan and the Hsia dynasty, was credited with the containment and control of the Great Flood. Hsieh, the Tzu clan's ancestor, was in some versions of Shang predynastic history an official at Yü's court and assisted him in controlling the flood. T'ang, founder of the Shang dynasty, was, according to *Shih Chi* (*Historical Memoirs* by Ssu-ma Ch'ien of the early first century B.C.), a man of such virtue that birds and beasts voluntarily entered his hunting net, even though the net was open on all sides. But T'ang had also performed meritorious deeds: once he threw himself into a fire in order to ensure the sucess of a rain-making ceremony; mercifully the rain came and put out the fire before T'ang was roasted. As for the Chi clan of the Chou dynasty, its ancestor, Hou Chi, was the beneficent hero who brought to his people millet, beans, and other crops.

The legendary kings who reigned before the Three Dynasties were culture heroes in their own right, at least in the telling of the people who wrote the accounts of their ancestors' lives, mostly in the late Chou period or during the Han dynasty. The most prominent of the heroic deeds of the Three Sovereigns and the Five Emperors are those attributed to the Yellow Emperor (Figure 18). He was the first great warrior among the sage ancestors: he fought Ch'ih Yu, a rival for supremacy, and defeated him at Chuo-lu (in Hopei), in the first great battle in Chinese history. He was also credited with the invention of the carriage and boat, the bronze mirror, housing, the cooking pot and the steamer, the crossbow, and a kind of football. Other inventions were attributed to the officials of his court: writing was supposedly devised by Ts'ang Chieh, music by Ling Lun, the Celestial Stems and Terrestrial Branches (the two sets of cyclical signs for the calendar) by Ta Jao, and medical texts by Lei Kung and Chi Po.[15]

14. Bernhard Karlgren, "Legends and cults in ancient China," *Bulletin of the Museum of Far Eastern Antiquities* 18 (1946).

15. Yuan K'o, *Chung-kuo Ku-tai Shen-hua* (Ancient myths of China) (Peking: Chung-hua, 1960), p. 136.

18. Portrait of Huang Ti, the Yellow Emperor,
from the second-century mural at Wu Liang Tz'u.

3

SHAMANISM AND POLITICS

One day around 500 B.C., King Chao (reigned 515–489 B.C.) of Ch'u, one of the hegemonic states of the Spring-and-Autumn period, was in a contemplative mood after reading one of the ancient documents in *Shu*. The document, "Lü hsing," was allegedly an edict issued to the marquis of Lü by King Mu of the Chou dynasty, perhaps in the late eleventh century B.C. It told of the great sage Ti Shun, who "commissioned Ch'ung and Li to cut the communication between heaven and earth." Puzzled, King Chao turned to his minister and asked, "If it had not been thus, would the people have been able to ascend to heaven?"

A myth of the "severence of heaven-earth communication" was then supplied by the minister, as recorded in *Kuo Yü*, a fourth-century B.C. text:

> Anciently, men and spirits did not intermingle. At that time there were certain persons who were so perspicacious, single-minded, and reverential that their understanding enabled them to make meaningful collation of what lies above and below, and their insight to illumine what is distant and profound. Therefore the spirits would descend into them. The possessors of such powers were, if men, called *hsi* (shamans), and, if women, *wu* (shamanesses). It is they who supervised the positions of the spirits at the ceremonies, sacrificed to them, and otherwise handled religious matters. As a consequence, the spheres of the divine and the profane were kept distinct. The spirits sent down blessings on the people, and accepted from them their offerings. There were no natural calamities.
>
> In the degenerate time of Shao-hao (traditionally put at the twenty-sixth century B.C.), however, the Nine Li threw virtue into disorder. Men and spirits became intermingled, with each household indiscriminately performing for itself the religious observances which had hitherto been conducted by the shamans. As a consequence, men lost their reverence for the spirits, the spirits

44

violated the rules of men, and natural calamities arose. Hence the successor of Shao-hao, Chuan-hsü [Figure 19], charged Ch'ung, Governor of the South, to handle the affairs of heaven in order to determine the proper place of the spirits, and Li, Governor of Fire, to handle the affairs of Earth in order to determine the proper places of men. And such is what is meant by cutting the communication between Heaven and Earth.[1]

This myth is the most important textual reference to shamanism in ancient China, and it provides the crucial clue to understanding the central role of shamanism in ancient Chinese politics. Heaven is where all the wisdom of human affairs lies. As Motse, the late-Chou philosopher, said, "The ghosts and spirits are wiser than the sages by as much as the sharp-eared and keen-sighted surpass the deaf and blind."[2] Access to that wisdom was, of course, requisite for political authority. In the past, *everybody* had had that access through the shamans. Since heaven had been severed from earth, only those who controlled that access had the wisdom — hence the authority — to rule. Shamans, therefore, were a crucial part of every state court; in fact, scholars of ancient China agree that the king himself was actually head shaman.[3]

If we look again at the meritorious deeds of the founders of the Three Dynasties, we find that all of their deeds were to some degree magical, supernatural. The Great Yü was powerful enough to stem the flood, and his gait — the so-called "Yü gait" — was later adopted as a special gait used by shamans.[4] T'ang, as we have seen, made rain through a ceremony, and Hou Chi had a special ability to make his crops grow fatter and faster than those of other farmers. These traditional beliefs have been well confirmed by the oracle bone inscriptions of the Shang dynasty, which show that the king was indeed the head shaman:

In the oracle bone inscriptions are often encountered inscriptions stating that the king divined or that the king inquired in connection with wind- or rain-storms, rituals, conquests, or hunts. There are also statements that "the king made the prognostication that . . . ," pertaining to weather, the border regions, or misfortunes and diseases; the only prognosticator ever recorded in

1. Quotations are from Derk Bodde, "Myths of ancient China," in *Mythologies of the Ancient World*, ed. Samuel N. Kramer (New York: Doubleday, 1961).

2. *The Ethical and Political Works of Motse* (London: Probsthain, 1929), p. 212.

3. Ch'en Meng-chia, "Myths and Magic of the Shang Dynasty" (in Chinese), *Yenching Journal of Chinese Studies* 20 (December 1936): 485–576; Li Tsung-t'ung, *History of Ancient Chinese Society* (in Chinese) (Taipei: Hua-kang, 1954), pp. 118–125; and Yang Hsiang-k'uei, *Studies of Ancient Chinese Society and Ancient Chinese Thought* (in Chinese) (Shanghai: Jen-min, 1962). Yang characterized the Ch'ung-Li myth by saying, "The kings severed communication between heaven and the people, and they took as their monopoly the great right of communicating with God" (p. 164).

4. Ch'en Meng-chia, "Myths and Magic of the Shang Dynasty," pp. 535–536.

19. Portrait of Chuan Hsü from the second-
century mural at Wu Liang Tz'u.

the oracle bone inscriptions was the king . . . There are, in addition, inscriptions describing the king dancing to pray for rain and the king prognosticating about a dream. All of these were activities of both king and shaman, which means in effect that the king was a shaman.[5]

The king, of course, was not the only shaman; he was assisted by many religious figures, all of whom may not have been strictly "shamanistic." The term "shaman" may be used here in the sense used by Arthur Waley: "In ancient China intermediaries used in the cult of Spirits were called *wu*. They figure in old texts as experts in exorcism, prophecy, fortune-telling, rain-making and interpretation of dreams. Some *wu* danced, and they are sometimes defined as people who danced in order to bring down Spirits . . . They were also magic healers and in later times at any rate one of their methods of doctoring was to go, as Siberian shamans do, to the underworld and find out how the Power of Death can be propitiated. Indeed the functions of Chinese *wu* were so like those of Siberian and Tungus Shamans that it is convenient . . . to use shaman as a translation of *wu*."[6]

The best-known evidence of ancient Chinese shamanism is in *Ch'u Tz'u* (*Elegies of Ch'u*), an anthology of seventeen pieces of poetry mostly attributed to Ch'ü Yüan (c. 340–278 B.C.) of Ch'u. One of the pieces is the "Chiu ko" ("The Nine Songs"), in which "male and female shamans, having first purified and perfumed themselves and dressed up in gorgeous costumes, sing and dance to the accompaniment of music, driving the gods down from heaven in a sort of divine courtship."[7] An example of this "divine courtship" can be seen in the following lines from "Yün chung chün" (The Lord Within the Clouds"):

> We have bathed in orchid water and washed our hair with perfumes,
> And dressed ourselves like flowers in embroidered clothing.
> The God has halted, swaying, above us,
> Shining with a persistent radiance.
> He is going to rest in the House of Life.
> His brightness is like that of the sun and moon.
> He yokes to his dragon car the steeds of god:
> Now he flies off to wander around the sky.
> The god had just descended in bright majesty,
> When off in a whirl he soared again, far into the clouds.
> He looks down on Chi-chou and the lands beyond it;

5. Ch'en Meng-chia, "Myths and Magic of the Shang Dynasty," p. 535.

6. Arthur Waley, *The Nine Songs: A Study of Shamanism in Ancient China* (London: Allen & Unwin, 1955), p. 9.

7. David Hawkes, *Ch'u Tz'u: The Songs of the South* (Oxford: Clarendon Press, 1959), p. 35.

There is no place in the world that he does not pass over.
I think of my lord with a heavy sigh,
And sad thoughts trouble my heart very sorely.[8]

The imagery here is like that of a love poem; it is clear that the basic role of a shaman (or shamaness, as in this poem) was that of an intermediary who used alluring dance and music to induce the deity to descend (Figure 20). Was shamanism a practice that extended beyond Ch'u and earlier than the fourth century B.C., Ch'ü Yüan's time? The answer is undoubtedly yes, but evidence from earlier times and other places is not as explicit as that found in *Ch'u Tz'u* and requires further analysis. First, there is the above-mentioned passage in *Kuo Yü* (probably slightly earlier than Ch'ü Yüan), pertaining to King Chao of the same Ch'u state, who reigned 515–489 B.C. There are also numerous — twenty-three, to be exact[9] — references to *wu*-shamans in *Shan Hai Ching*, portions of which were compiled during the earlier parts of the first millennium B.C.,[10] including references to special mountains where the shamanistic ascent was to take place (Figure 21). Chow Tse-tsung has also presented an interesting argument suggesting that "*wu*-shamans originated the practice of medicine" and attributing medical knowledge to ancient kings and sages."[11]

The best evidence for shamanism in ancient China before *Ch'u Tz'u*, however, consists of artifacts from the Shang dynasty — namely, oracle bone inscriptions and representations of animals in art. Art is the subject of Chapter 4; following is a brief discussion of oracle bones.[12]

The inhabitants of North China during the third millennium B.C. were the first people anywhere to use the shoulder blades of animals for divination (by heating them and interpreting the resultant cracks).[13] By

8. Translated by Hawkes, *Ch'u Tz'u*, p. 37.

9. *Index du Chan Hai King* (Université de Paris: Centre d'Études Sinologique de Pékin, 1948), pp. 26–27.

10. Meng Wen-t'ung, "A brief discussion on the date of writing of *Shan Hai Ching* and its place of origin" (in Chinese), *Chung-hua Wen-shih Lun-ts'ung* 1 (August 1962): 43–70.

11. Chow Tse-tsung, "Ancient Chinese *wu* shamanism and its relationship to sacrifices, history, dance-music, and poetry," *Tsing Hua Journal of Chinese Studies*, n.s., 12 (December 1979): 1–59.

12. For a detailed treatment of the subject, see David N. Keightley, *Sources of Shang History*, (Berkeley: University of California Press, 1978).

13. See K. C. Chang, *The Archaeology of Ancient China* (New Haven: Yale University Press, 1977), pp. 175–180, 189.

20. A depiction of the descent of the "Lord Within the Clouds," described in the poem in *Ch'u Tz'u*.

21. Group of *wu*-shamans, as illustrated in *Shan Hai Ching*.

the time of the Shang in the middle of the second millennium B.C. this practice had reached its height with the addition of three new features: the widespread use of turtle shells as well as shoulder blades, the sophisticated preparation of the bones (they were incised with a series of hollows and grooves prior to the divination, to facilitate heating), and the carving of inscriptions on the bones (Figures 22, 23). [14] After the fall of the Shang, the use of bones for oracles and the practice of inscribing them were continued by the Chou on a reduced scale until these customs died out soon afterward. But the custom of burning animal shoulder blades for divination continued in a large part of the northern hemisphere of both the Old and the New Worlds until relatively recent times. [15]

The Shang oracular activities took place largely at the royal court under the king's direct supervision, for his ritual and political purposes exclusively, and a large number of officials — including religious figures fitting the *wu*-shaman definition — were involved. First, the bones — about half of them shoulder blades of cattle (*Bos exiguus*) and water buffalo (*Bubalus mephistopheles*) and the other half plastral shells of turtles — were obtained, mostly by importation; the turtle shells were often from species found in South China (*Ocadia sinensis, Mauremys mutica, Cuora* species). Presumably the scarcity of the bones added something to their quality as instruments of communication. The bones were carefully prepared — scraped, polished, perhaps soaked and dried, finally chiseled to produce rows of grooves and hollows. During the ritual, the diviner applied heat at the bottom of the grooves and hollows to produce hairline cracks on the opposite surface of the bone. These cracks were interpreted to provide answers to the questions that were put to the ancestors. The king himself sometimes would bring the question to the diviner, but more often he asked the question through a mediating "inquirer." The cracks were interpreted by a "prognosticator," a role in which the diviner himself could have doubled but which the king himself often performed.

How the cracks were interpreted we do not know. The degree of "auspiciousness" as shown by the cracks was sometimes noted with inscriptions near them, but the notations do not seem to correlate

---

14. *Shang Civilization* (New Haven: Yale University Press, 1980), pp. 32–33.

15. For a succinct description of the practice of scapulimancy in historic times throughout the northern hemisphere from Europe to North America, see Keightley, *Sources of Shang History*, pp. 4–5.

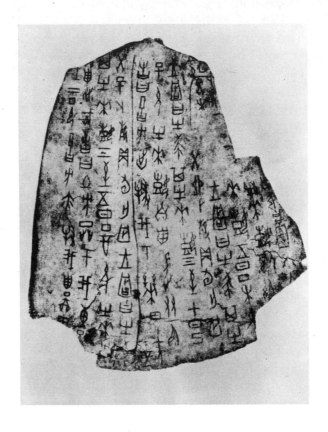

22. Inscribed shoulder blade of the Shang
dynasty.

23. Inscribed turtle shell of the Shang dynasty.
Length is about 25 centimeters.

systematically with the shapes and angles of the cracks.[16] Possibly the diviner had to enter into a different verbal or mental contract with the ancestors each time a heating took place,[17] but if so the details of such contracts, if any, have been lost. After the divination, an inscription sometimes would be made next to the cracks to record the question asked and, occasionally, the answer given. From these inscriptions we know that the king would turn to his ancestors for confirmation or approval before undertaking such actions as building a new town, engaging in a battle, going on a hunt or a journey, or performing a ritual in a particular way. He might ask his ancestors to tell him about his fortune in the coming night or the coming week, about a dream he had had, about the birth of a consort's child, about disease or even a toothache. Scholars who study these inscriptions have been able to find out much about the religious and ritual life of the kings, as well as about various other aspects of Shang culture and society.

Was Shang divination an act of Shang shamanism? The inscriptions make it clear that inquiries were directed to long-departed ancestors, and that the diviner served as an intermediary. The inscriptions often contain the word *pin*, which in later classical texts usually means to receive as a guest or to be a guest. In the oracle bone inscriptions, the word is often placed between the word for king and the name of a specific ancestor or of Ti, the Supreme God. A phrase consisting of these elements is sometimes interpreted as "the king receives as a guest a specific ancestor," or "the king receives as a guest the Supreme God."[18] But more likely it means that the king "called upon" a departed ancestor or God. *Shan Hai Ching* states that "Ch'i went up to *pin* heaven three times," making it clear that *pin* refers to the human chief going to the deity rather than the other way around. In any event, there was a Shang ritual that enabled the king and the spirits to be together, presumably brought about by some kind of middleman. The act of divination was intended, similarly, to bring the middleman diviner and the spirits together.

16. Chang Ping-ch'üan, "Divination cracks on the oracle bones at Yin-hsü and related problems" (in Chinese), *Annals of Academia Sinica* 1 (June 1954): 231–245.

17. According to Lin Sheng, "Investigation and study of divination by sheep scapulae among the Ta-lu people of the Yi ethnic group in Yung-sheng county, Yunnan" (in Chinese), *K'ao-ku* 1964 (2): 98–102, divination by heating the shoulder blades of sheep is still practiced among the Ta-lu people in Yung-sheng county, Yunnan province, in southwestern China. Before each such ritual, the diviner in his prayer indicates what kinds of cracks he anticipates — whether he expects an auspicious or inauspicious response. When cracks are produced, he interprets them accordingly.

18. Shima Kunio, *Inkyo Bokuji Kenkyū* (A study of the oracle bone inscriptions from Yin Hsü) (Tokyo: Kyūko Shoin, 1958), p. 201.

The descent of the spirits or the ascent of the shaman or the king was achieved in a manner not altogether clear. Music and dance were apparently part of the ceremony. Alcoholic drinks were possibly involved: the Shang were notorious drinkers, and many bronze ritual vessels were designed to serve alcoholic beverages. Did the alcohol or other substances bring about a trance, during which the shaman engaged in imagined flight? Possibly, but there is as yet no concrete evidence for this. The role of animals in the ritual art of the Shang may provide significant clues.

4

ART AS THE PATH TO AUTHORITY

Animal designs are a well-known feature of the decorative art of Shang and early Western Chou bronzes.[1] Animal motifs reached their height of development during the An-yang phase of the Shang, but an early form of animal mask, at least the eyes and a facial outline, is already apparent on middle Shang bronzes, and it may even be related to some of the much earlier decorative designs on black pottery and on jades in prehistoric cultures of the eastern coast.[2] By late Shang (An-yang) and early Western Chou times, animal motifs had become highly complex and varied. A list of such animals designs compiled by Jung Keng includes: the *t'ao-t'ieh* design, the *t'ao-t'ieh* design composed of banana leaves, the *k'uei* design, the double-headed *k'uei*, the triangular *k'uei*, the dragon with two tails, the curling dragon, the plain dragon, *ch'iu* design, the rhinoceros, the owl, the hare, the cicada, the silkworm, the turtle, the fish, the bird, the phoenix, the elephant, the deer, the curling *k'uei*, the *k'uei* in a leaf, and the frog and algae design.[3] Other common animals

1. Cheng Te-k'un, "Animal in prehistoric and Shang China," *Bulletin of the Museum of Far Eastern Antiquities* 35 (1963): 129–138; Li Chi, "Hunting records, faunistic remains, and decorative patterns from the archaeological sites of An-yang," *Bulletin of the Department of Archaeology and Anthropology, National Taiwan Universtiy* 9/10 (November 1957): 10–20.

2. Hayashi Minao, "A view on the animal mask designs of ancient China" (in Japanese), *Museum* 301 (April 1976): 17–28; Hayashi Minao, "The jade culture before the Yin dynasty"(in Japanese), *Museum* 334 (January 1979): 4–16; Wu Hung, "A group of early jade and stone sculptures" (in Chinese), *Mei-shu Yen-chiu* 1 (February 1979): 64–70; Jessica Rawson, *Ancient China: Art and Archaeology* (London: British Museum, 1980), p. 78.

3. Jung Keng, *A Comprehensive Study of Shang and Chou Bronze Ritual Vessels* (in Chinese) (Peking: Harvard-Yenching Institute, 1941).

seen on An-yang bronzes are oxen, water buffalo, sheep, tigers, bears, horses, and boars.

Clearly, there are two kinds of animals in these designs. On the one hand, there are real-world animals: rhinoceros, owl, hare, cicada, silkworm, turtle, fish, bird, elephant, tiger, deer, frog, ox, water buffalo, sheep, bear, horse, and boar. On the other hand, there are many which do not occur in the real world and which must be referred to by the mythological names found in ancient texts. The following are particularly prominent (see Figure 24).

1. *T'ao-t'ieh.* The third-century B.C. book *Lü-shih ch'un-ch'iu* (in the chapter entitled "Hsien-shih lan") refers to "the *t'ao-t'ieh*, conspicuous on Chou [or Hsia, in another version] dynasty *ting*-tripods, which has a head but is bodiless. It tries to devour a man but before it can swallow him his own body is destroyed. [This image was used] to illustrate the principle of just deserts." On the basis of this description, traditional Chinese antiquarians since the Northern Sung Dynasty (twelfth century) have identified the mythicized animal mask commonly encountered on Shang and Chou bronzes as the *t'ao-t'ieh*.

2. *Fei-yi.* *Shan Hai Ching*, in the chapter entitled "Pei-shan ching," contains a description of "a snake with one head but two bodies, which is called *fei-yi* and which when seen causes drought in the land." (Contrast this with the *t'ao-t'ieh*, which may not have a body at all.) Li Chi suggests the use of the name *fei-yi* for the design that consists of an animal head at the center in full face with two elongated bodies, each extending to one side.[4]

3. *K'uei.* According to *Shuo-wen* (compiled A.D. 100) *K'uei* is the name of a kind of "divine spirit that looks like a dragon with a single foot." This beast is described in *Shan Hai Ching* ("Ta-huang tung ching") as "looking like a bull, black, hornless, with a single foot. When it enters into and emerges from the water, there will be a windstorm. It shines like the sun and moon and its voice sounds like thunder . . . The Yellow Emperor once captured one. He used its skin to make a drum and beat the drum with the bone of a thunder beast. The sound could be heard beyond five hundred *li*." In *Chuang Tzu* (c. 300 B.C.), in the chapter entitled "Ch'iu shui," a *k'uei* is described in conversation with a *hsüan*, another divine animal, perhaps a millipede, as he talks about his jumping around with "a single foot." Traditionally, antiquarians have used the name *k'uei* to refer to the design that shows the profile of a mythological (that is, uniden-

---

4. Li Chi, *A Study of the Bronze Chia-type Vessels Excavated from Yin-hsü* (in Chinese) (Nankang: Academia Sinica, 1968), pp. 69–70.

24. Mythical animals in Shang bronze decorative designs. Top row: *T'ao-t'ieh*. Second row: *Fei-yi*. Third row: *K'uei*. Bottom row: *Lung*.

tifiable) animal with only a single visible leg, foot, or claw. (The same design with two or more legs, feet, or claws would be called a *lung*.)

4. *Lung*. The most common mythical animal mentioned in ancient texts is the *lung*, or "dragon," but a precise description of its morphology is lacking. *Shuo-wen* describes it as "the chief of all scaled reptiles. It is sometimes dark, sometimes bright; sometimes small, sometimes big; sometimes short, sometimes long. It ascends to heaven at the spring equinox, and dives into the water at the autumn equinox." Wen Yi-to, in a treatise discussing such concepts as "the intertwined *lung*" or "the pair of *lung*," gives the following description: "The *lung* resembles a horse, so the horse is sometimes referred to as the *lung*. Sometimes the *lung* resembles a dog, which is thus also called *lung* . . . In addition, a kind of *lung* with scales resembles the fish, a kind with wings resembles the bird, and a kind with horns resembles the deer. As to the various kinds of reptiles that are often confused with the *lung*, they need not even be mentioned."[5] Since the form of the *lung* is so flexible and varied, antiquarians have likewise used the term very flexibly: all animals in bronze designs that cannot be identified as real-world animals and that also cannot be referred to by the names of any of the other mythological creatures (such as *t'ao-t'ieh*, *fei-yi*, or *k'uei*) are thus *lung*, or dragons.

5. *Ch'iu*. The *ch'iu* is apparently a special kind of *lung* without horns according to the commentary of Wang Yi (early second century) on "Li sao."

These and other names for mythical animals are found in ancient texts, and modern scholars have adopted them to label specific animal designs on Shang and Chou bronzes. Have they applied the names correctly? If a person from the Shang or Chou were to read our antiquarian works, would he recognize these names and approve their usage? It is impossible to say.

However, several facts are indisputable as far as the animal designs on Shang and Chou bronze art are concerned. It is known that these designs occur in large numbers and constitute the majority of decorative designs in Shang and early Western Chou bronze art. They include a large variety of animals, both those that can be identified as real-world animals and those that can be described only with the names of mythological

5. Wen Yi-to, "A study of Fu-hsi" (in Chinese), in Wen Yi-to, *Mythology and Poetry* (in Chinese) (Peking: Chung-hua, 1956), p. 25.

animals in ancient texts. In addition, two other characteristics must be mentioned.

First, the animal designs on Shang and Chou bronzes often — though far from always — occur in pairs and are placed on the surface of the object in a symmetrical pattern. The basic decorative component is a band of animal designs that circles the vessel. The band is divided into units, often by flanges, each unit being filled with an animal in profile. When an animal profile is pointed toward the left, the animal profile in the adjoining unit on the left is often pointed toward the right, resulting in the joining together of two side views of the animal head, separated by the flanges at the center. Viewed from the center line, the two animal profiles may be described either as a single animal split into two halves, each spreading sideways, or as two animals joined together along the median line of the face. Thus, the *t'ao-t'ieh* and the *fei-yi* can both be looked at either as two animals joined together or as a single animal split apart. We will return to this point below.

Second, on a small number of Shang and possibly early Western Chou bronzes, both human and animal figures occur together. The best known of these are the pair of *yu* in the Sumitomo[6] and the Musée Cernuschi[7] collections. A little man is depicted on the *yu* as hugging a tiger-like animal, and his head is placed under the open mouth of the animal. The man-beast theme is also seen on a bronze *kuang*[8] and a bronze knife[9] in the collection of the Freer Gallery of Art, Washington, D.C.; on the handle of a square *ting* found in the 1930s in the eastern sector of the Shang royal cemetery in An-yang;[10] on the face of a bronze ax in the tomb of Shang's Lady Hao at Hsiao-t'un, An-yang, excavated in 1976;[11] and on the surface of a bronze *tsun* unearthed in Fu-nan, Anhwei, in 1957.[12] In addition to the juxtaposition of man and beast, these bronze artifacts share other decorative features: the animals' mouths are open and the

6. Umehara Sueji, *The Collection of Old Bronzes of Sumitomo* (in Japanese) (Kyoto: Sen'oku Museum, 1971), pp. 62–65.

7. Vadime Elisséeff, *Bronzes archaïques chinois au Musée Cernuschi*, vol. 1 (Paris: L'Asiathèque, 1977), pp. 120–131.

8. John A. Pope, et al., *Freer Chinese Bronzes*, vol. 1 (Washington, D.C.: Freer Gallery of Art, 1967), no. 45.

9. According to photographs taken by the author.

10. Ch'en Meng-chia, "Yin dynasty bronzes" (in Chinese), *K'ao-ku Hsüeh-pao* 1954 (7): 15–59.

11. "The excavation of Tomb No. 5 of Yin-hsü, An-yang" (in Chinese), *K'ao-ku Hsüeh-pao* 1977 (2): pl. 13.2.

12. Ko Chieh-p'ing, "Bronze artifacts of Shang dynasty date found in Fu-nan, Anhwei" (in Chinese), *Wen-wu* 1959 (1): inside cover.

human head is below or close to the mouth; the human head or body is perpendicular to the axis of the animal head or body; and the animal designs all appear to be depictions of the tiger. There are important variations. A single animal is shown with the man in the Kyoto, Paris, and Washington pieces, whereas the three other pieces all feature two animal profiles facing each other, with the human head flanked by their open jaws; on some pieces the human is represented by only a head, whereas on the other pieces the human figure is complete with a body; on the *yu* pieces the human and the animal embrace, but on all other pieces they are separate (Figure 25).

Any interpretive theory aiming to account for the meaning of the animal design on Shang and Chou bronzes should explain all of the above characteristics and not just some of them. In other words, the issue of the animal design involves not a single question but a series of questions: Why did the bronze makers of the Shang and Chou use animal designs on their decorations? What functions did these designs serve in Shang ideology? Why was there such variety? Why do the figures often appear in pairs? Why do they sometimes occur together with humans? Why do man and beast appear in such distinctive formal relationships?

The Meaning of Animal Designs

Is there "meaning" in the animal designs on Shang and Chou bronzes? That is, was there an iconographic meaning invested in the animal forms by Shang and Chou artists? Most students of ancient Chinese bronzes believe that there is such a meaning, and past studies — too many to be enumerated here — have pointed either to familiar totems or to mythical deities that are represented by specific animals; but there are few Shang and Chou documents linking specific designs with specific totems or deities. In contrast, a minority opinion (with forceful advocates) holds that animal forms developed out of geometric forms, as an afterthought, as it were, and that therefore they have no meaning. The most frequently quoted lines advocating such a position are those of Max Loehr:

If the ornaments on Shang bronzes came into being as sheer design, form based on form alone, configurations without reference to reality or, at best, with dubious allusions to reality, then, we are almost forced to conclude, they cannot have had any ascertainable meaning — religious, cosmological, or mythological — meaning, at any rate, of an established, literary kind. Quite possibly these ornaments were iconographically meaningless, or meaningful

61

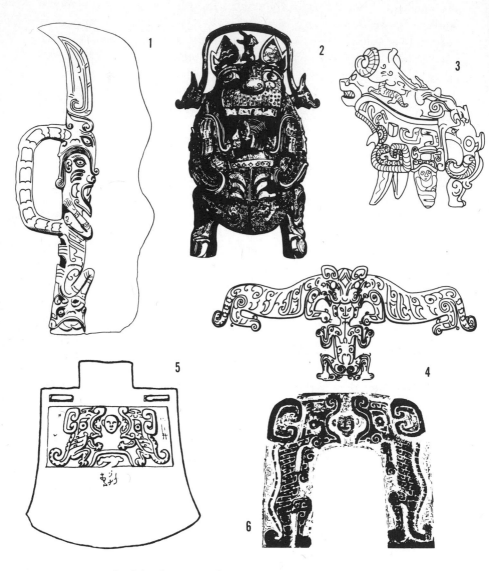

25. Man-beast motif in Shang bronze art.
(1) Freer Gallery knife. (2) *Yü* in the Sumitomo
collection, Kyoto. (3) *Kuang* in Freer Gallery.
(4) Motif on the *tsun*-beaker found in Fu-nan,
Anhwei. (5) Ax from Tomb 5 at Yin-hsü, An-
yang. (6) Motif on handle of four-legged cauldron
found at Yin-hsü.

only as pure form — like musical forms and therefore unlike literary defini-
tions.[13]

The opposing positions are clear, and a resolution easily suggests itself.
The problem, I believe, can be approached from two directions
simultaneously. On the one hand, we should be able to ascertain the
historical sequence of the development of the animal designs to see if indeed geometric form alone has temporal precedence. On the other hand,
we can propose an iconographic theory that is convincingly based on
facts. With regard to the first point, we can simply state that zoomorphic
decorative designs not only occurred as early as the earliest known
decorative designs on ancient Chinese bronzes, but may be traceable
even to the neolithic period. With regard to the second point, we need to
devise a theory of meaning that scholars may be reasonably expected to
find convincing. Such a theory should result from a straightforward
reading of the textual and archaeological facts, and it should take into account *all* of the characteristic features of animal designs described above.
I believe that such a theory exists.

In fact, explanations of the meaning of both the bronze ritual vessels
and their animal motifs are furnished by the ancient Chinese themselves
in pre-Ch'in texts. Recall the description of the myth of the separation of
heaven and earth, as related in *Kuo Yü*. The Chinese original of the
passage that was quoted in Chapter 3 used two words, *wu* (animal offerings) and *ch'i* (ritual vessels), in such a way as to make it clear that the
shamans and shamanesses were instrumental in the communication between heaven and earth, or between ancestral spirits and other deities
and living people, and also that both the vessels and the *wu*-animal offerings were a part of the paraphernalia essential for the performance of the
heaven-earth communication ritual.

If the bronze vessels were designed to help in the ritual of bringing the
dead and the living together, might not the animal designs on them have
been an essential part of the paraphernalia? This question is clearly
answered in *Tso Chuan*, third year of Duke Hsuan (606 B.C.). In that
year, King Chuang of Ch'u went on a military expedition against the
Jung tribe of Lu-hun. When he reached the Lo River he halted to view his
troops near the Chou capital in Lo-yang. King Ting of Chou sent Wang-
sun Man to welcome the King of Ch'u, who impudently asked Wang-sun
about the size and the weight of the *ting*-tripod, the royal symbol. Wang-
sun Man's pointed reply began as follows:

13. Max Loehr, *Ritual Vessels of Bronze Age China* (New York: The Asia Society, 1968),
p. 13.

Ting-tripods do not matter; virtue does. In the past when the Hsia dynasty was distinguished for its virtue, the distant regions put into pictures their distinctive *wu*, and the nine pastors sent in the metal of their provinces. The *ting*-tripods were cast, with representations on them of those *wu*. All the *wu* were represented, and [instructions were given] for the preparations to be made in reference to them, so that the people might know [the distinctions] between the helping and the harming spirits. Thus the people when they went among the rivers, marshes, hills, and forests did not meet with the injurious things, and the hill-spirits, monstrous things, and water-sprites did not meet with them [to do them injury]. Hereby a harmony was secured between the high and the low [or heaven and earth], and all enjoyed the blessings of heaven.[14]

This passage has been interpreted variously,[15] but the above translation represents a very simplified literal interpretation. To paraphrase, it means that the Hsia cast the bronze tripods and put the images of the *wu* on them so that living people would realize which animals were helping people to cross from earth to heaven and which animals were unhelpful or even harmful. Thus, Wang-sun Man as much as tells us that among the animals are some which are capable of helping the shamans and the shamanesses in their task of communicating between heaven and earth, and that the images of these animals were cast on ancient bronze ritual vessels. This is a relevant point in Wang-sun Man's reply to the King of Ch'u because he concludes by saying that the King of Chou is still very much in touch with heaven!

The key word in the *Tso Chuan* passage is *wu*, which is translated not as "objects" but as "animal offerings" or "animals to help in heaven-earth crossings." This reading is based on two facts. First, on the ancient vessels themselves we see not "objects" but animal images, which have to be the "representations on them of those *wu*" referred to in *Tso Chuan*. Second, the passage makes it clear that the purpose of the casting of tripods with *wu* images on them is such that "a harmony was secured between heaven and earth and all enjoyed the blessing of heaven," which conforms completely with the statement of *Kuo Yü* discussed earlier, concerning the function of the bronze vessels. If the bronze ritual vessels were a part of the shamanistic paraphernalia in the heaven-earth crossing, it should come as no surprise that images of animals who were helpers in this task were cast on the vessels.

14. Based on the translation in James Legge, *The Chinese Classics*, vol. 5 (Oxford: Clarendon Press, 1895), p. 293.

15. An example is Chiang Shao-yuan, *A Study of Travels in Ancient China* (in Chinese) (Taipei: Shang-wu, 1935; rpt. 1966).

Can the word *wu* be used in this way? The word appears in *Tso Chuan* some five or six dozen times and was used in various ways, but "animals with power" or "animal offerings" was the meaning on many occasions. Under the entry for the tenth year of Duke Ting (500 B.C.) we read that "the armor of the Shu-sun Shih are [decorated with] *wu*." According to what we know of ancient armor, the decor could only be animal designs, not "objects." Under the entry for the thirty-second year of Duke Chuang (662 B.C.) is the following passage:

> In autumn, in the seventh month, there was the descent of a spirit in Hsin. Kung Huei asked Kuo, the historiographer of the Interior, the reason for it, and he replied: "When a state is about to flourish, intelligent spirits descend in it, to survey its virtue. When it is going to perish, spirits also descend in it, to behold its wickedness . . . " The king then asked what should be done in the case of this spirit, and Kuo replied, "Present to it its own proper *wu*, which are those proper to the day on which it came."[16]

Wu here is usually translated as "offerings," which varied according to the spirits involved and the days in question. These documentary data, recalling the passage in *Kuo Yü*, show that the sacrificial animals were the same ones which had the power to help the shamans and shamanesses in their communication task, and that to make animal offerings was a concrete means of achieving communication between heaven and earth, the dead and the living.[17] We thus come to the inevitable conclusion that the animal designs on Shang and Chou bronzes are iconographically meaningful: they are images of the various animals that served as the helpers of shamans and shamanesses in the task of communication between heaven and earth, the spirits and the living.

Earlier, in connection with *lung*, or dragon, we saw the phrase "a pair of *lung*." This appears repeated in *Shan Hai Ching*, where the term is invariably associated with agents bringing messages back and forth between heaven and earth. The chapter entitled "Ta-huang hsi ching" contains an account of the well-known deed of Ch'i (or K'ai), the second sovereign of the Hsia dynasty: "Beyond the sea in the southwest, south of

16. Based on translation in Legge, *The Chinese Classics*, p. 120.
17. See Fu Ssu-nien, "Postscript to Mr. Ch'en P'an's essay discussing the story about the Duke shooting fish by arrow at T'ang in the *Ch'un Ch'iu*" (in Chinese), *Bulletin of the Institute of History and Philology, Academia Sinica*, 7 (December 1938): 194–197. The character *wu* (which is a different character from the *wu* meaning shaman) in the oracle inscriptions of the Shang has not been absolutely identified and is sometimes confused with the character *li*, meaning plow; see Li Hsiao-ting, *Collected Interpretations of Characters in the Oracle Bone Inscriptions* (in Chinese), Institute of History and Philology, Academia Sinica, Monograph no. 50 (rpt. Taipei, 1970), pp. 317–330.

the Red River, and west of the shifting sands, a man wears two green snakes on his ears and rides on two *lung*-dragons, and his name is K'ai, the Lord of Hsia. K'ai ascended to heaven three times to have an audience [with God] and he descended with the [poems and songs] '*Chiu-pien*' and '*Chiu-ko*.'"[18] The same figure is seen also in the "Hai-wai hsi ching" chapter, where he is again described as riding on two *lung*-dragons. Clearly K'ai was a hero who brought heavenly music and poetry to the world, and in that role he was a shaman helped by two snakes and two dragons.

These dragons and snakes were also standard equipment for God's agents of the four directions (Figure 26):

East: "In the east is Kou Mang, who has the body of a bird and the face of a human, and rides on two *lung*-dragons" ("Hai-wai tung ching").

West: "In the west is Ju Shou, who wears a snake on his left ear and rides on two *lung*-dragons" ("Hai-wai hsi ching").

South: "In the south is Chu Jung, who has the body of a beast but the face of a human, and rides on two *lung*-dragons" ("Hai-wai nan ching").

North: "In the north is Yü Chiang, who has the face of a human but the body of a bird. He wears two green snakes on his ears and has two green snakes under his feet" ("Hai-wai pei ching"). Another version reads: "with black body, hands, and feet, riding on two dragons" ("Hai-wai pei ching").

In his commentary to *Shan Hai Ching*, Kuo P'u (276–324) said that Kou Mang had been sent by Shang Ti, the Supreme God, to bring to Duke Mu of Ch'in an extra nineteen years of life, and that Ju Shou was the deity who served Ti Shao-hao. The dragons and the snakes presumably were related to their role as God's agents, bridging His world and man's. It should be noted that *Shan Hai Ching*, in which references to *lung*-dragons appear frequently, has been characterized as "a book for shamans in the ancient times."[19] The only other book in which the same

18. See also the lines: "In the Nine Variations and Nine Songs of Ch'i / The house of Hsia made revelry and knew no restraint," in "Li sao," translated in David Hawkes, *Ch'u Tz'u: The Songs of the South* (Oxford: Clarendon Press, 1959), p. 26.

19. Yuan Hsing-p'ei, "A preliminary exploration of the *Shan Hai Ching*" (in Chinese), *Chung-hua Wen-shih Lun-ts'ung*, September 1979 (3): 7–35.

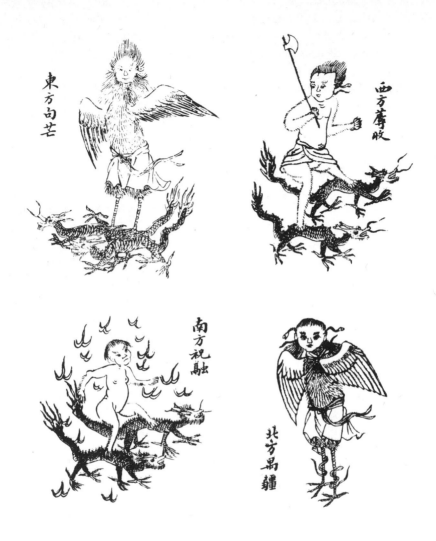

東方句芒

西方蓐收

南方祝融

北方禺疆

26. The agents of the four directions, as illustrated in *Shan Hai Ching*. Upper left: Kou-mang of the East. Upper right: Ju-shou of the West. Lower left: Chu-jung of the South. Lower right: Yu-chiang of the North.

reference to the two *lung*-dragons appears is *Ch'u Tz'u*,[20] another late Chou volume tied to the shamanistic tradition.[21] Such data on the role of dragons and snakes in the shamanistic task of ascension add weight to the view that the animal designs on Shang and Chou bronzes also represent agents between man and the other world.

Even though ancient documents such as *Kuo Yü, Tso Chuan, Shan Hai Ching*, and *Ch'u Tz'u* date from the late Chou dynasty, it is generally believed that they contain some facts from Shang and earlier Chou histories. In any event, the religious and cosmological concepts found in them should to some extent be continuous with those from earlier periods. Insofar as the shamanistic task of bridging worlds and the role of animal helpers are concerned, evidence for these is found in oracle bone inscriptions of the Shang. The oracular predictions themselves were, in fact, made with the bones of animals, which were truly instruments of heaven-earth communication. In addition, the inscriptions show that Shang Ti or Ti, Supreme God on High, was believed to have been served by a number of officials, including "the messenger phoenix."[22] The animal images on the Shang and Chou bronzes thus provide direct documentation for such beliefs.

All these reconstructed or speculative roles for vessels and for animals indeed exist in those modern-day societies with shamanism which ethnographers have been able to observe. As Mircea Eliade pointed out, "The shamans also have divinities peculiar to them, unknown to the rest of the people, and to whom they alone offer sacrifices . . . The majority of these familiar and helping spirits have animal forms. Thus among the

20. Also depicted as riding on two dragons was Ho Po, the God of the Yellow River, See the poem "Ho Po," in "Chiu-ko":

> I wander with you by the Nine Mouths of the river
> When the storm wind rises and lashes up the waves.
> I ride a water chariot with a canopy of lotus;
> Two dragons draw it, between two water-serpents.

Translated in David Hawkes, *Ch'u Tz'u*, p. 42. For additional details on Ho Po, see Wen Ch'ung-yi, "A study of the Ho Po in 'Chiu ko'" (in Chinese), *Bulletin of the Institute of Ethnology, Academia Sinica* 9 (Spring 1969): 139–162.
21. See Ling Shun-sheng, "Bronze drum designs and the 'Chiu ko' in *Ch'u Tz'u*" (in Chinese), *Annals of Academia Sinica* 1 (June 1954): 403–417; Fujino Iwatomo, *A Treatise on the Literature of the Shamanistic Tradition* (in Japanese) (Tokyo: Daigaku Shobō, 1969); Chan Ping-leung, "*Ch'u Tz'u* and the shamanism in ancient China," diss., Ohio State University, 1974.
22. Ch'en Meng-chia, *A Comprehensive Description of the Oracle Bone Inscriptions from Yin Hsü* (in Chinese) (Peking: Science Press, 1956, p. 572).

Siberians and the Altaians they can appear in the form of bears, wolves, stags, hares, all kinds of birds (especially the goose, eagle, owl, crow, etc.), of great worms, but also phantoms, wood spirits, earth spirits, hearth spirits, and so on."[23] As pointed out by scholars and their shamanistic informants, "The shaman's power rests in his ability to throw himself into a trance at will . . . The drum and dance simultaneously elevate his spirit and conjure to him his familiars — the beasts and birds, invisible to others, that have supplied him with his power and assist him in his flight. And it is while in his trance of rapture that he performs his miraculous deeds. While in his trance he is flying as a bird to the upper world, or descending as a reindeer, bull or bear to the world beneath."[24] One of the common ways of summoning the shaman's animal familiars is to offer such animals for sacrifice, from whose bodies the animal spirits are released and undertake their ascent (Figure 27).

Following is an interesting example of a shaman's use of animal spirits to lift him up and over barriers. A Nisan shamaness, a Manchu of Chinese Manchuria, was described in a long narrative as being on a long journey. When she

reached the bank of the Red River . . . she looked around [but] there was no boat to ferry her across and she did not even see the shadow of a person. Consequently there was nothing else to do: she began to murmur, beseeching the spirit:

> *Eikuli yekuli* Great eagle
> *Eikuli yekuli* circling the sky,
> *Eikuli yekuli* silver wagtail
> *Eikuli yekuli* circling the sea,
> *Eikuli yekuli* malicious snake
> *Eikuli yekuli* slithering along the river bank,
> *Eikuli yekuli* eight pythons
> *Eikuli yekuli* going along the Jan River —
> *Eikuli yekuli* Young lord, I Myself
> *Eikuli yekuli* want to cross
> *Eikuli yekuli* this river.
> *Eikuli yekuli* All you spirits
> *Eikuli yekuli* lifting me, ferry me across.
> *Eikuli yekuli* Hurry!
> *Eikuli yekuli* Reveal your power!
> *Eikuli yekuli*

23. Mircea Eliade, *Shamanism: Archaic Techniques of Ecstasy* (Princeton University Press, 1964), pp. 88–89.

24. Joseph Campbell, *The Masks of God: Primitive Mythology* (New York: Viking Press, 1959), p. 257.

Then throwing her drum into the water the shaman herself stood on top of it, and like a whirlwind she crossed the river in an instant.

Later, at the end of the journey, she reached the city she was heading for. But the gates were closed. She again murmured her chants to conjure up a great soaring bird, a sandalwood kingfisher, an oakwood badger, nine snakes, eight pythons, a small tiger, a wolverine, a golden wagtail, a silver wagtail, a flying hawk, a lead eagle, a many-colored eagle, and vultures. "When she finished, all the spirits rose up in flight and became like clouds and fog."[25]

Such contemporary accounts of shamanism do not by themselves prove anything for the Shang and Chou Chinese three thousand years ago, but observations of modern-day shamanistic activities and the roles of animal familiars in these activities confirm that what the ancient Chinese told us and what we have reconstructed on the basis of archaeological and textual evidence are actually workable systems in human society.

These examples also show that animal familiars are none other than the common animals which the shamans and their people know in everyday life. As Li Chi pointed out, "[the] majority of the animal patterns employed by the decorative artists of this period, whether carving a stone, casting a bronze, inlaying a wooden article, moulding a clay object, polishing a piece of jade, had originally an indigenous and naturalistic background."[26] The animals he named as providing decorative motifs for Shang art include the deer, ox, buffalo, goat, sheep, antelope, rhinoceros, elephant, bear, horse, tiger, and boar, as well as birds, reptiles, insects, amphibians, fishes, and worms. Probably they all served as shamans' helpers and, if the above argument is valid, they served sacrificial purposes. As to the mythological animals such as the *t'ao-t'ieh*, *fei-yi*, *k'uei*, and *lung*, they were surely not real-world animals, but apparently they were transformed from naturalistic prototypes of the ox, sheep, tiger, and reptiles. Li Chi wrote that

> the inlaying technique . . . must have given the artists, when manipulating these mechanically cut units of shells, a sense of freedom never enjoyed by the wood-carvers, who had only stumps of wooden timber to deal with. It must be especially true, when the inlaying technicians were faced with the problem of how to delineate a plastic object on a flat background. Their solution was to split a tri-dimensional animal body into two equal halves and arrange the split units in the most symmetrical fashion on the plane of a two-dimensional

25. Margaret Nowak and Stephen Durrant, *The Tale of the Nisän Shamaness: A Manchu Folk Epic* (Seattle: University of Washington Press, 1977), pp. 62–63, 67.

26. Li Chi, "Hunting Records," p. 12.

27. Animal spirits ascending in rituals, as depicted by the Chukchee of Siberia. Left: Autumn sacrifice to the Sea Spirit. The Sea Spirit and his wife are shown in the upper right corner. Shamans are performing inside the tent, with ritual vessels on the floor. On the left, animal spirits are ascending; one is a bird and another is a fox. Right: A funerary rite. Sacrificial animals are shown being offered at right; their spirits are ascending to the residence of the death deity. The deceased is shown knocking on his door.

28. Images of Pu T'ing Hu Yü (right) and Yin Yin Hu (left) from *Shan Hai Ching*.

decorative field. The success of this new arrangement created in the mind of these artists a sense of freedom that led them to indulge their imagination further in this direction; they started to manipulate the different parts of the whole body after this fashion and began to take liberty to transplant the part of the body of one animal on that of the other and vice versa, or exaggerate one part of the animal at the expense of the other part; such imaginative wanderlust was restricted only by the boundary of the decorative field. The decorative artists must have been perfectly delighted with this new sense of freedom; and soon, the sculptors, the potters, the jade carvers, and the bronze founders all followed suit. So the tiger's head may be attached to a simian body, and a pair of horns may be planted on a human skull . . . Nevertheless, it is important to observe, the elementary materials with which these artists worked were all taken from their direct contact with the physical world.[27]

Other Features of Animal Designs

Earlier we noted two characteristic features of Shang and Chou animal designs — their frequently symmetrical arrangement on the surface of the object, and the occasional distinctive juxtaposition of human and animal forms. Can the above hypothesis concerning the meaning of animal motifs also explain these additional features?

One of the earliest references to the man-beast relationship in ancient Chinese bronze art was made in 1908 by Lo Chen-yü, who described the Sumitomo piece as depicting "a beast that has grabbed a man and acts as if to devour him."[28] Jung Keng referred to it as the *t'ao-t'ieh shih jen yu*, or "the *yu* wine goblet showing a *t'ao-t'ieh* devouring a human,"[29] a term that seems to have become accepted usage among Chinese antiquarians. The term is based on a reading of the man-beast relationship as one of antagonism or worse — a reading that is consistent with the role assigned to the *t'ao-t'ieh* in *Lü-shih ch'un-ch'iu*, which tells of its *shih jen* or practice of "devouring humans."[30]

A closer look at the seven man-beast objects known, however, reveals no convincing evidence that the act of devouring is what has been represented. On the Sumitomo and Cernuschi *yu*-vessels the man is shown hugging the beast, his feet firmly planted on the beast's hind paws; and the Fu-nan and An-yang pieces depict a human face seen frontally, wedged between the gaping mouths of two beasts but not within them.

27. Li Chi, "Hunting Records," p. 16. Compare T'an Tan-chüng, "The composition of the *t'ao-t'ieh* design" (in Chinese), *Bulletin of the Institute of History and Philology, Academia Sinica*, special no. 4 (1960): 274.
28. Lo Chen-yü, *Yung-lu Jih-cha* (Daily notes at Yung-lu), in *Ch'i-ching K'an Ts'ung-k'an* (1937), bk. 9, p. 3.
29. Jung Keng, *A Comprehensive Study*, pp. 419–420.
30. This is pointed out by Tung Tso-pin, in "The *yu* vessel with the *t'ao-t'ieh*-devouring-man design" (in Chinese), *The Mainland Magazine (Ta-lu Tsa-chih)* 9 (September 1954): 35.

We certainly should seek alternative interpretations for the gaping beast's mouth and for the placement of the human head beneath or beside it.

The man-at-the-gaping-mouth-of-a-beast motif occurs throughout the world. As Nelson Wu stated,

> One common idiom in religious art is the motif of the serpent, an animal associated with water and hibernation. Frequently a composite animal form is employed for this purpose, and the mystical makara [of India] is the most commonly found. These notions may be behind the carving of the Sarpa Gumpha (Serpent Cave) at Udayagiri whose entrance is underneath the cobra hood of the naga motif. Nearby is the Bagh (Tiger) Gumpha, which is entered through the wide open mouth of the beast. Similar usage in separating one world from another is common in other cultures. Temple XXII in Copan, Honduras, with its serpent entrance way, and the *t'ao-t'ieh* motif of Chinese bronzes are other examples half a world apart.[31]

The view that the gaping mouth of the beast may be an archetypal symbol separating one world (such as the world of the dead) from another (such as the world of the living) fits well with our discussion here, which argues that the animal functions precisely as the shaman's helper in the crossing from one world to another. Seen in this light, the human depicted could be none other than the shaman, shown as he is being aided in his journey.[32] The gaping mouth could be an archetypal motif traceable to man's paleolithic past, but in the immediate context of ancient China it could also signify the animal's breath, which the ancient Chinese believed was a cause of wind. Wind was another essential instrument in heaven-earth commination.

Shan Hai Ching furnishes information with regard to the placement of beasts on either side of the human head and to the origin of wind in animal breath. It contains many references to the shaman's wearing of snakes on one or both ears (see under "Hai-wai hsi ching," "Hai-wai pei ching," "Hai-wai tung ching," "Ta-huang tung ching," "Ta-huang nan ching," "Ta-huang hsi ching," and "Ta-huang pei ching"). A most interesting deity (or shaman) is referred to in "Ta-huang nan ching": called Pu T'ing Hu Yü, he wears snakes on both ears, has snakes at each foot, and has a companion called Yin Yin Hu, who produces the wind from his mouth (Figure 28). The origin of wind in animal breath is described in

31. Nelson I. Wu, *Chinese and Indian Architecture* (New York: George Braziller, 1963), p. 25.

32. This is not to be confused with the idea that the *t'ao-t'ieh* represents the shamanistic mask, although our shamans could very well have worn *t'ao-t'ieh*-shaped masks. See Jordan Paper, "The meaning of the t'ao-t'ieh," *History of Religions* 18 (August 1978): 18–41; Carl Hentze, "Eine Schamanentracht in ihrer Bedeutung für die Altchinesische Kunst," *IPEK* 20 (1963): 55-61.

connection with the mythical creature Chu-yin, or Chu-lung: "The deity of Chung Mountain is called Chu Yin. When it opens its eyes there is day, and when it closes its eyes there is night. When it blows breath the winter comes, and when it sucks in air the summer comes. It does not drink, eat, or breathe; when it does breathe, there comes wind. Its body is a thousand *li* long, placed east of Wu-ch'i. It has a human face and a snake body, and its color is red" ("Hai-wai pei ching"). This creature is probably the prototype of the creator Pan Ku, who is described in *Wu-yun Li-nien Chi* by Hsü Cheng (third century) as one "whose breath brings forth the wind and the clouds." As mentioned above, Shang oracle inscriptions refer to the phoenix as God's messenger, and a single character designates both wind and phoenix in the Shang script. Just as the four directions each have a special agent riding on two dragons, so does each also have a wind.[33] The animals in bronze art may have produced wind out of their gaping mouths, thus helping the shamans in their ascent. The combination of the shamanistic image, his animal assistants, and the gaping mouth as the source of the lifting wind on a single bronze vessel depicts the act of communication — or even causes that act — in its most complete form.

Whatever the direct link may be between the animal mouth and the lifting wind, the placement of the human (possibly shamanistic) head below or beside the animal mouth clearly suggests the closeness (*not* the antagonism) of the man-beast relationship. As pointed out by Wu and, much earlier, by Carl Hentze,[34] the man-beast motif is a major shared element in the ancient arts of China and of Mesoamerica. Among the ancient Aztecs, for example, every newborn child was assigned an animal by a shaman; the animal would for the rest of the child's life serve as protector, helper, companion, or alter ego.[35] In ancient art the alter ego is often shown as an animal carried on the person's back or enveloping the human head in its open mouth. In fact, the alter ego motif is circum-Pacific in its distribution.[36] This does not necessarily mean that all alter ego motifs had a single historical origin; but the situation in these other

33. Ch'en Pang-huai, *Yin dynasty social historic data* (in Chinese) (Tientsin: Jen-min, 1959), entry under Names of Four Direction Winds.

34. Carl Hentze, *Objets rituels, croyances et dieux de la Chine antique et de l'Amérique* (Anvers: De Sikkel, 1936); idem, *Die Sakralbronzen und ihre Bedeutung in den Fruehchinesischen Kulturen* (Antwerp: De Sikkel, 1941); idem, *Bronzegerät, Kultbauten, Religion im ältesten China der Shang-Zeit* (Antwerp: De Sikkel, 1951).

35. Maguel Leon-Portilla, *Aztec Thought and Culture* (Norman: University of Oklahoma Press, 1965).

36. Douglas Fraser, *Early Chinese Art and the Pacific Basin, A Photographic Exhibition* (New York: Intercultural Arts Press, 1968).

cultures furnishes useful clues to the interpretation of the Chinese case. To regard the man as shaman and the beast as his helper is certainly a view consistent with the alter ego motif. New World art also sheds light on the fact that on Chinese bronzes the beasts depicted with humans are all tigers. In early cultures of the New World the jaguar was the alter ego for the members of the highest class. In the Shang dynasty, as previously noted, the kings were sometimes called the highest shamans.[37] Very possibly these man-beast motifs on ancient artifacts of China could represent not only the shaman bridging worlds but the king himself or one of his close kinsmen.

Finally, we come to the symmetrical pairing of animals in Shang and Chou designs, which is consistent with the textual references to *liang lung*, or "a pair of dragons." An interpretation of this phenomenon depends on the formulation of an important principle in the composition of the design. Are the animal designs that are seen frontally the result of splitting a single animal and then spreading the halves laterally on a flat surface, or of joining two animal profiles at the center of the face? The former is apparently the predominant view. H. G. Creel's speculation on this is among the earliest: "The peculiarity of the *t'ao-t'ieh* is that it represents the head of the animal as if it were split in two, and the severed halves laid out on either side, being joined in the middle on a line with the nose . . . If we take the two halves together they give a perfectly good *t'ao-t'ieh*, seen from the front, with two eyes, two ears, two horns, and the lower jaw represented twice. But let the reader cover the right-hand half of the picture with his hand. The left half is now a dragon seen from the side."[38] The "lower jaw" referred to is more likely an extension of the upper jaw, for the lower jaws of animals are rarely if ever depicted. But the principle speculated upon here is consistent with the common practice of splitting images as seen in the wood carvings of the northwest coast Indians of North America.[39]

The opposite view, however, is equally plausible: the *t'ao-t'ieh* and the *fei-yi* are interpreted as two animal profiles joined together at the median axis of the face. Earlier we quoted Li Chi's speculation that the *t'ao-t'ieh* face originated in inlay art and split images. In later writings, Li Chi appeared to incline toward the opposite sequence, at least as another possibility. In his studies of the decorative animal bands seen on bronze

37. Ch'en Meng-chia, "Myths and magic in the Shang dynasty" (in Chinese), *Yenching Journal of Chinese Studies* 20 (December 1936): 532–576.

38. Herrlee G. Creel, *The Birth of China* (New York: Frederick Ungar, 1937), p. 115.

39. Herrlee G. Creel, "On the origins of the manufacture and decoration of bronzes in the Shang period," *Monumenta Serica* 1 (1935/36): 64.

ting-tripods from Hsiao-t'un, An-yang, he arranged the animals in a sequence (which he calls logical, if not chronological), beginning with two independent dragons facing each other and ending with a characteristic *fei-yi* band with a single frontally viewed face at the center (Figure 29).[40]

The two interpretations of the origins of the *t'ao-t'ieh* and *fei-yi* do not have to be mutually exclusive: both sorts of development could actually have taken place. Any definitive answer must be based on much additional artifactual dating to demonstrate the actual chronology of the many variations of the motif. The whole issue of origin has considerable relevance to Shang cosmology and some bearing on the meaning of animal designs. Claude Lévi-Strauss, for example, saw the technical need to spread out the three-dimensional animal head onto a two-dimensional surface as the probable cause of the dualism in Shang cosmology.[41] A plausible contrary view could be that the artistic dualism on Shang bronzes is merely one component, an integral part, of a dualism that permeated Shang institutions and Shang thought.

A number of other dualistic phenomena are present in both archaeological and textual data pertaining to the Shang. (1) The palace-temple foundations of the Shang capital at Hsiao-t'un have a layout consisting of an eastern row and a western row arranged along a north-south axis.[42] (2) The royal cemetery of the Shang dynasty, where the last eleven kings of the dynasty are believed to be buried, is divided into a western sector of seven tombs and an eastern sector of four tombs, separated by a distance of more than a hundred meters.[43] (3) The oracle inscriptions were engraved on turtle shells in such a way as to place "positive" inquiries on one side of the shell and "negative" inquiries on the opposite side of the shell (see Figure 23).[44] (4) The ritual institutions of the Shang kings at An-yang, according to Tung Tso-pin's studies of oracle bone inscriptions, belonged to two schools, the Old School and the New School.[45] (5) According to Bernhard Karlgren's statistical studies, Shang

40. Li Chi, *Studies of the Bronze Ting-shaped Vessels Excavated from Yin-hsü* (in Chinese) (Nankang: Institute of History and Philology, Academia Sinica, 1970), pp. 81–82.

41. Claude Lévi-Strauss, "Split representation in the art of Asia and America," in Lévi-Strauss, *Structural Anthropology* (New York: Basic Books, 1963), pp. 245–268.

42. Tung Tso-pin, *Sixty Years of Oracle Bone Inscriptions Studies* (in Chinese) (Taipei: Yi-wen, 1965), p. 30.

43. Kao Ch'ü-hsün, "The royal cemetery of the Yin dynasty at An-yang," *Bulletin of the Department of Archaeology and Anthropology, National Taiwan University* 13/14 (November 1959): 1–9.

44. Chou Hung-hsiang, *Examples of Symmetrical Divinations in the Oracle Bone Inscriptions* (in Chinese) (Hong Kong: Wan-yu, 1969).

45. Tung Tso-pin, "Preface" (in Chinese), in *Yin-hsu Wen-tzu Yi-pien* (Institute of History and Philology, Academia Sinica, 1948).

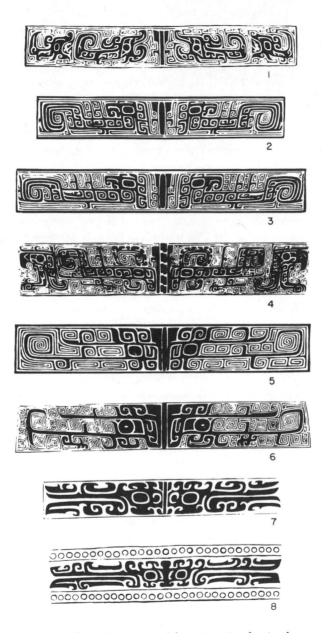

29. A "logical sequence," from 1 to 8, of animal design development. The designs are taken from decorative bands on *ting*-tripods of the Shang, excavated at Yin-hsü.

77

bronze decorative motifs can be divided into A and B styles, depending on their pattern of co-occurrence on the same vessel.[46]

On the basis of these phenomena I proposed in 1964 that dualism is an important key to the study of Shang society and, also, that the dualism of Shang institutions is probably closely related to the division of the royal house into halves.[47] I have discussed the issue of royal dualism at some length elsewhere;[48] a general description will be sufficient here. The royal family was divided into ten groups, which were named after the ten Heavenly Stems and which were ritual, political, and endogamous units. The kingship rotated among the ten groups, but the groups were split into two major divisions, one dominated by the stem-Yi group and the other dominated by the stem-Ting group. This division of the royal family suggests explanations for the layouts of the palace-temple complex at Hsiao-t'un and the royal cemetery at Hsi-pei-kang, and it may explain the alternation of the Old and New Schools of Shang rituals.

The issue confronting us is not the nature of the Shang system of kingship, which cannot be described adequately here, but whether or not the hypothesis presented here can satisfactorily explain the "two-dragon" principle of Shang and Chou art. In my opinion it can, precisely because of our understanding of Shang kingship. When the royal house was divided into two, the royal ancestors were presumably arranged similarly in the other world. When the shamans crossed from one world to the other in the service of the royal family, they had to take both halves of the royal house into consideration, and it was logical to include a pair of animal helpers in the ritual. When the shamans were riding on "two dragons," they in a sense had one foot in each world, attempting to achieve an appropriate social and political balance corresponding to that in the human world.

Conclusion

The above interpretation of animal motifs in Shang and Chou art not only enables us to understand them in the context of their religious roles,

46. Bernhard Karlgren, "New studies in Chinese bronzes," *Bulletin of the Museum of Far Eastern Antiquities* 9 (1937).

47. K. C. Chang, "Some dualistic phenomena in Shang society," *Journal of Asian Studies* 24 (November 1964): 45–61.

48. K. C. Chang, "A new study of the temple names of the Shang dynasty kings" (in Chinese), *Bulletin of the Institute of Ethnology, Academia Sinica* 15 (Spring 1963): 65–94; idem, "The days of sacrifice to Wang Hai and Yi Yin and the rules of kingship of the Shang dynasty" (in Chinese), *Bulletin of the Institute of Ethnology, Academia Sinica* 35 (Spring 1973): 111–127.

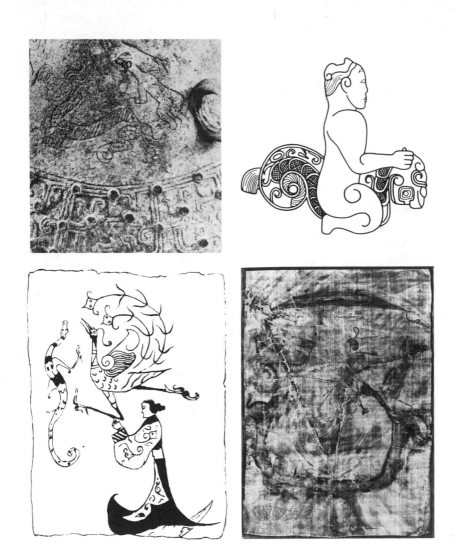

30. Shamans and the animals they were driving in
Eastern Chou art. Upper left: Decorative design
on the upper part of a *hu*-vessel. Upper right:
Jade figure from a tomb in Lo-yang. Lower left:
Figures from a silk painting of the Ch'u
civilization found in Ch'ang-sha, Hunan. Lower
right: Another silk painting from Ch'ang-sha.

but it also explains why ritual bronzes of the Shang and Chou decorated with animal designs were highly valued as the symbolic treasure of the political houses. Clearly, if animals in Shang and Chou art were the principal medium employed by shamans to communicate with heaven, then possession of animal-styled ritual bronzes meant possession of the means of communication. Possessors of such means of communication were invested with wisdom and thus with power. The more animals, the better; and for this reason, as *Tso Chuan* relates, "the distant regions put into pictures their distinctive *wu*," and all their *wu* were cast into the royal bronzes. Presumably, the royal shamans and the regional shamans each had their hierarchies of animal helpers.

The shamanistic interpretation of animals in Shang and Chou art also suggests that the Shang and Chou shamans, who used animals as their assistants or agents, did indeed engage in "flights" into the ancestral or spiritual world. This role played by animals was by no means confined to the Shang and early Chou; a number of Eastern Chou art objects (Figure 30) depict human figures in the act of "driving" animals. These may well represent Eastern Chou shamans with their animal agents, although the positional relationship between shaman and animal in these images is not identical to that shown in earlier man-beast motifs.

5

WRITING AS THE PATH TO AUTHORITY

What was the momentous event in ancient China that caused "millet grains to rain from heaven and ghosts to wail at night"? According to *Huai Nan Tzu* (compiled in the second century B.C.), these marvels took place on the occasion of Ts'ang Chieh's invention of writing (Figure 31). Ancient Chinese mythology is full of catastrophes but describes very few happy incidents. Why did the beginning of writing assume such earth-shaking importance? The written record held the secret of the governance of the world; the inscriptions were identified with the information they contained because when writing began they themselves were part of the instruments of the all-important heaven-earth communication. In other words, the medium was at least part of the message. The "media people" — the possessors of the power of the written word — were the first people in Chinese history who earned their living by acquiring and transmitting knowledge in the form of written words.

If Ts'ang Chieh indeed invented writing — "inspired by the claw prints of birds," in the telling of a number of legends of the late Warring-States period (450–220 B.C.) — we have as yet discovered no written account of his life or any trace of his tomb. Recent archaeological evidence, however, has shown that Chinese writing underwent a long and gradual process of development and that it perhaps originated in more than one area independently.

At a large number of prehistoric sites incised marks, apparently of a symbolic character, have been found on pottery vessels or potsherds (Figure 32). These sites date from the early Yang-shao Culture (older than 5000 B.C.) to just before the historic periods (whose dates of inception varied according to the region), and they are found throughout

像 頡 倉

31. A fanciful portrait of the legendary Ts'ang
Chieh.

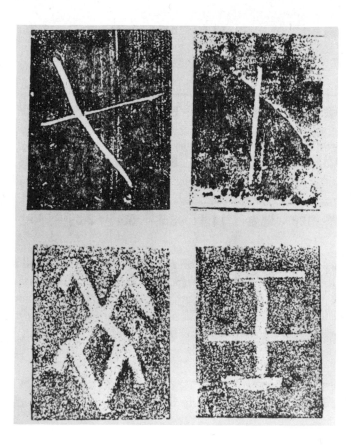

32. Marks found on pottery vessels at the Yang-shao Culture site at Chiang-chai, in Lin-t'ung, Shensi.

China, from the entire Yellow River valley to the southern and eastern coastal areas. These sites are as follows:[1]

1. Yang-shao Culture (5000–3000 B.C.): Pan-p'o, Sian, Shensi; Wu-lou, Ch'in-tu-chen, Sian, Shensi; Chiang-chai, Lin-t'ung, Shensi; Hsin-yeh-ts'un, Ho-yang Hsien, Shensi; Liu-wan, Lo-tu, Chinghai
2. Ta-wen-k'ou Culture (4500–2500 B.C.): Ling-yang-ho, Chü Hsien, Shantung; Ch'ien-chai, Chu-ch'eng, Shantung
3. Lung-shan Culture (3000–2200 B.C.): Ch'eng-tzu-yai, Lung-shan-chen, Chi-nan, Shantung
4. Southeastern Coastal Cultures (2500–500 B.C.): Sung-tse, Shanghai; Ma-ch'iao, Shanghai; Liang-chu, Hang Hsien, Chekiang; Feng-pi-t'ou, Kao-hsiung, Taiwan; Pa-tzu-yuan and Pao-lou, Hai-feng, Kwangtung; Ta-wan, Lamma Island, Hong Kong; Shek-pik, Lantau Island, Hong Kong

There is no reason to expect the list to stop here, but the available data are sufficient to illuminate a few of the main characteristics of these marks. First of all, they appear singly and apparently were not strung together as written language. Second, these marks — incised on the pottery mostly before firing but occasionally after firing — appear on only a tiny percentage (less than one half of one percent in Li Hsiao-ting's counting)[2] of the pottery that has been found at each site. Third, there are only a very small number of different characters, and only a few of them are found at more than one site. According to Li Hsiao-ting's listing,[3] eighty-eight characters are found at all the prehistoric sites, and of these only sixteen have appeared at more than one site. There is not much that can be deduced from the above, except that there seems to have been a custom of marking the pottery for some reason under certain circumstances, a custom that was found throughout China. The recurrent characters could be coincidences, or they could be the same symbols meaning the same things at different places.

More important than the recurrence of these marks at two or more prehistoric sites is, I believe, the fact that some of these marks are identical to characters in the inscriptions of the earliest historic dynasties, the Shang and Chou. This could mean that even though the prehistoric

1. K.C. Chang, *Shang Civilization* (New Haven: Yale University Press, 1980), p. 243.
2. Li Hsiao-ting, "Another discussion on the prehistoric pottery scripts and the problem of the origin of Chinese characters" (in Chinese), *Bulletin of the Institute of History and Philology, Academia Sinica* 50 (September 1979): 458.
3. Li Hsiao-ting, "Another discussion," pp. 478–483.

pottery marks cannot be characterized as writing, as individual characters they furnished at least one source for the earliest Chinese writing. It is therefore worth investigating the purpose of these marks, for we might then learn what aspect of their many activities the prehistoric Chinese (or Ts'ang Chieh) considered worthy of recording with symbols.

Potters' marks are widely found in both ancient and modern cultures throughout the world; careful studies have shown that in many instances they were signatures of individual potters or of their shops.[4] In the Chinese case, it might be useful to begin an investigation of such prehistoric marks by ascertaining the purpose of incised marks on the pottery of Shang and later periods, for they may suggest the same function in prehistory. I believe that the overwhelming majority of these ceramic marks, both Shang and prehistoric, were markers and emblems of families, lineages, clans, or divisions of these.

Several students of Chinese archaeology maintain that the marks incised before firing of the pottery probably identified the individual maker, whereas those scratched on after firing probably identified the owner. It is true that many Lin-tzu pottery inscriptions appear to be names of individual potters or shops,[5] but this pottery was produced during the late Chou period, when potters and other craftsmen were full-time specialists and tradesmen. Yang-shao pottery, in contrast, was almost certainly not manufactured by specialists; pottery making in the village of Pan-p'o was probably a domestic activity of every household. There is evidence, at the archaeological site at Pan-p'o, that particular pottery inscriptions tended to be concentrated in particular areas of the village: "We have found that many similar signs occur in the same storage pits or in the same area. For example, an analysis of the provenance data of the most common sign, the single vertical stroke, shows that most of the 72 pieces bearing this sign were found at six loci that basically adjoin one another in an area of just over a hundred square meters. In storage pit H341 we found two sherds with the same sign. All five Z-shaped signs clustered within two grid squares."[6] Similar indica-

4. See, for examples, Daniel Potts, "The potter's marks of Tepe Yahya," *Paléorient* 7 (February 1981): 107–122, for the Near East; Christopher B. Donnan, "Ancient Peruvian potters' marks and their interpretation through ethnographic analogy," *American Antiquity* 36 (October 1971): 460–466, for Peru; Michael B. Stanislawski, Ann Hitchcock, and Barbara B. Stanislawski, "Identification marks on Hopi and Hopi-Tewa pottery," *Plateau* 48 (Spring 1976): 47–65, for the modern Hopi Indian of Arizona.

5. Ku Ting-lung, *A Catalogue of Ancient Pottery Writings* (in Chinese) (Peking: National Peking Academy, 1936), p. 8.

6. Shih Hsing-pang, et al., *Hsi-an Pan-p'o* (Peking: Science Press, 1963), p. 198.

tions occur at the Feng-pi-t'ou site in Taiwan, where sherds with incised X-signs cluster in a single area on the southern edge of the village.[7] This phenomenon suggests that the so-called numerals that several scholars have read in these prehistoric signs[8] were probably not more than signs that happened to be identical to some of the numerals that were developed much later. In early historic China, the numerals 1, 2, 3, and 4 were simply characters with 1, 2, 3, or 4 short strokes; 5 was an X-mark; and 7 was simply a cross-mark. These forms are common at many sites. The other Chinese numerals, 6, 8, and 9, were more arbitrarily designated, and these have not been found to occur in any prehistoric pottery inscriptions. As Li Chi asked, with regard to the pottery inscriptions at Hsiao-t'un, "How is it that some numerals (7) are seen so frequently, others (1, 3, 4) are rare, and still others (2, 6, 8, 9) are not found at all?"[9] Since single or multiple strokes, crosses, and X's are signs commonly used in many cultures to identify and to distinguish lots, these probably were simply meant to indicate that pottery vessels were of this lot or that lot, possibly in relation to some social divisions. Characters identifiable as names or emblems went a step further, identifying pottery vessels with specific, named groups; but in principle there is little difference between these and lot marks.

This interpretation of some or most prehistoric and Shang pottery inscriptions — as markers or emblems of the social groups using the pottery — is quite consistent with the usage of many inscriptions on Shang bronzes (Figure 33).[10]

The fact that writing — at least some of the writing — of ancient China was possibly derived from emblematic symbols (symbols of kin groups invested with political and religious power) would lead us to expect that

7. K. C. Chang, et al., *Fengpitou, Tapenkeng, and the Prehistory of Taiwan*, Yale University Publications in Anthropology, no. 73 (New Haven: Yale University, 1969), pl. 54.

8. Li Hsiao-ting, "A speculation on the origin of the Chinese writing based on observations on pottery scripts from prehistory and early history" (in Chinese), *Nanyang Journal of Chinese Studies* 3 (1969): 1–28; Kuo Mo-jo, "The dialectic history of ancient scripts" (in Chinese), *K'ao-ku* 1972 (3): 2–13; Cheng Te-k'un, "The development and uses of the numerals in ancient China" (in Chinese), *Journal of the Chinese University of Hong Kong* 1 (March 1973): 37–58; Ho Ping-ti, *The Cradle of the East* (Hong Kong and Chicago: Chinese University of Hong Kong Press and University of Chicago Press, 1976), ch. 6.

9. Li Chi, *Pottery of Hsiao-t'un* (in Chinese) (Taipei: Institute of History and Philology, Academia Sinica, 1956), p. 124.

10. K. C. Chang, "A preliminary report on a comprehensive study of the form, decoration, and writing of Shang and Chou bronzes" (in Chinese), *Bulletin of the Institute of Ethnology, Academia Sinica* 30 (Autumn 1972): 239–315; Li Xuegin, *The Wonder of Chinese Bronzes* (Peking: Foreign Languages Press, 1980), pp. 49–50.

0 ____ 5 cm

33. Emblems cast on bronze vessels found in
Tomb 18 at Yin-hsü, dating from the Shang
dynasty.

aspects of ancient Chinese writing had intrinsic power. What we know about the association of writing and power in ancient China seems, actually, to bear out this expectation. The power of the written word came from its association with knowledge — knowledge from the ancestors, with whom the living communicated through writing; which is to say, knowledge from the past, whose wisdom was revealed through its medium.

It is clear from the texts of the Eastern Chou period that there were people who possessed knowledge of the past and who therefore were able to draw from past experience and predict the outcome of contemplated actions. Such ability was obviously of value to the rulers of the various states. In *Tso Chuan* we find that the duke of Lu and the rulers of other states in the Spring-and-Autumn period (771–450 B.C.) often consulted their ministers or officials for advice, and that often the ministers or officials would cite the behavior of ancient sage kings as the authority for their own advice. Such citations are recorded in *Tso Chuan* under the entries for 710, 686, 662, 656, 655, 654, 651, 645, 641, 636, 627, 609, 606, 603, 598, 594, 593, 589, 570, 565, 564, 546, 541, 540, 535, 533, 525, 523, 516, 514, 511, and 504 B.C. Most of the events referred to pertain to the early history of the Chou dynasty: nine references to the Conquest of Shang, eight references to model kings or exemplary behavior in the early Chou, five to Wen Wang, and two to the end of the Western Chou. In addition, there are five references to ancient history across the dynasties, four to the early sages Yao and Shun, three to Hsia dynasty kings, and only one to a Shang king. For the Warring-States period (c. 450–220 B.C.), *Meng Tzu (Mencius)* may be used as an example: its 260 sections are full of advice that Mencius gave to his rulers; in at least fifty-eight of these sections he cited the authority of the figures of the past. On ten occasions he cited Emperor Yao, on twenty-nine occasions Emperor Shun, on eight occasions the Great Yü, on ten occasions King T'ang of the Shang dynasty, on seventeen occasions the predynastic kings of the Chou, and on twelve occasions kings of the early Chou dynasty. It appears that by Eastern Chou times there had evolved a standard generalized history of the previous fifteen hundred years, and that the behavioral patterns evident in this history enabled men of learning to foretell the future.

The ability to predict was, of course, the central purpose of the traditional historiography of China. To the question "Why was the study of the past so esteemed and what sorts of value were ascribed to it?" Arthur F. Wright gave the following answers: "One is that the successes and failures of the past provide sure guidance for one's own time . . . The Confucian tradition, as it developed, perpetuated the injunction to study the past as a repository of relevant experience. A second justification for history was . . . [that] to study history was to understand in clusters of concrete instances how men had fared when they lived in accord with or in defiance of the moral injunctions of the classics."[11] Ancient historiographers were thus invested with moral authority which no rulers dared ignore, precisely because this authority was based on knowledge of the past — namely, knowledge of the acting out and the consequences of these "moral injunctions of the classics."[12]

It must be pointed out that historiographers had no monopoly on the knowledge of the past; Mencius, for one, was not a historiographer himself. They were — especially prior to the Eastern Chou period, when knowledge spread to a much larger number of the members of the elite — simply the one group of people in ancient China who had convenient access to knowledge. Or to put it another way, possession of knowledge was the key to past and future, and historiography was merely the one official avenue to it. Possession of knowledge of the past could actually be equated to literacy, and access or nonaccess to the written record was the key to predictive power in the ancient art of governance; for in Motse's words, "The sources of our knowledge lie in what is written on bamboo and silk, what is engraved on metal and stone, and what is cut on vessels to be handed down to posterity."[13]

Therefore, to identify the class or classes of people who possessed knowledge of the past in the Shang and early Chou is to determine who had access to writing in those periods, and to chronicle the beginning of such classes is to chronicle the beginning of writing. Although the available data enable us to speculate on some of their implications, on these important issues we are largely ignorant. Between the prehistoric potters' marks (which could not yet be called writing) and the Eastern Chou classics, the principal written materials consist of the oracle bone inscriptions of the Shang and early Chou dynasties and the bronze in-

11. Arthur F. Wright, "On the uses of generalization in the study of Chinese history," in *Generalization in the Writing of History*, ed. Louis Gottschalk (Chicago: University of Chicago Press, 1963), pp. 37–38.

12. Li Tsung-t'ung, "The institution of the office of historiographer, with a discussion on the reverence for tradition" (in Chinese), *Bulletin of the College of Arts, National Taiwan University* 14 (November 1965): 119–157.

13. Translated in Mei Yi-pao, *The Ethical and Political Works of Motse* (London: Probsthain, 1929), and quoted in Tsuen-tsuin Tsien, *Written on Bamboo and Silk* (Chicago: University of Chicago Press, 1962), p. v.

scriptions of the Shang and Western Chou dynasties. We can only speculate about who was responsible for these inscriptions.

The Shang oracle bone inscriptions are the occasional recordings of the oracular inquiries made on behalf of the kings and, infrequently, also the answers given by the ancestors. Very little is known about why these inscriptions were made.

> Contrary to what some scholars have supposed, the engravers did not carve the charge into the bone or shell before the cracking took place, but after. This suggests that the scapulimantic and plastromantic inscriptions were not simply regarded as prayers or magical letters forwarded to the spirits. The writing recorded not what was about to be divined but what had been. Its purposes, therefore, were at least partly historical and bureaucratic — to identify the topics, forecasts, and results for which the cracks had been formed.[14]

Since the oracular results presumably came from the wisdom of the departed ancestors, the recording of such results for future reference (or even generalizations) suggests that these inscriptions may have had the same purpose as the written records of later epochs; the possessors of the oracular knowledge may thus be the first known members of the "knowledge class." However, it is far from clear who these possessors were. We know only that there were several oracular functions: initiating the oracular inquiry on behalf of the king; carrying out the physical act of divining with bones and shells; reading the cracks and prognosticating; engraving the inscriptions; and filing the shells and bones in the archives for future reference.[15] Scholars of Shang oracle bone inscriptions are uncertain as to whether these functions were performed by separate individuals or, if not, how many specialists were involved. We do know that there were more names of inquirers than there were calligraphic styles, a fact that has led to the speculation that only a small number of specialized calligraphers-engravers were in existence at any one time.[16] Theoretically it is possible that the calligrapher was the only person who had to be literate and that the inquirers and the diviners needed only to concern themselves with the religious act. But the art of divining was presumably a continuous process; and if the pattern of ancestral answers was to be preserved in the inscribed archives, the diviners must presumably have helped with the keeping and the inter-

---

14. David N. Keightley, *Sources of Shang History* (Berkeley: University of California Press, 1978), p. 45.

15. Jao Tsung-yi, *A Comprehensive Study of the Diviners in the Yin Dynasty* (in Chinese) (Hong Kong: Hong Kong University Press, 1959), pp. 17–18.

16. Keightley, *Sources of Shang History*, pp. 48–49.

pretation of the records. In fact, the combination of the historiographic and the shamanistic roles in individuals would be in accord with the view of many historians that the earliest historiographers were also religious — possibly shamanistic — figures.[17]

Historiographic functions are also manifest in the inscriptions cast on many ritual vessels of the Shang and Chou dynasties. Eastern Chou people made it clear that such inscriptions were cast more for the benefit of the descendants than of the ancestors. "The philosopher Mo Tzu said that the reason for engraving inscriptions on vessels and cutting on metals and stone was the fear that if the perishable materials should rot and disappear, the descendants might not be reverent and obtain blessings."[18] Inscriptions of the Chou period often end with the phrase, "You descendants treasure and use this vessel forever and ever" (Figure 34). The inscriptions make it clear that the vessels were cast and inscribed often at the instigation of high officials who had received favors from the king or his lords or ministers; but we are unclear as to the process of literary composition and calligraphic execution. Presumably there were specialists in charge of these matters, and these specialists possessed the knowledge of historical patterns. A recently discovered *p'an*-basin bears a long inscription stating that the vessel was made by order of a historiographer named Ch'iang, whose lineage specialized in Tso Tz'e, "the making of bamboo books" (Figure 35).[19] The existence of such a specialist profession and its endowment with knowledge of the past would conform with the implications of the oracle bone inscriptions.

In sum, we have noted that historiographers were not the sole possessors of knowledge pertaining to past patterns (in fact, they are often depicted in historical texts as being rather passive, insofar as giving advice to rulers is concerned) and that most of the media in which knowledge was transcribed no longer survive in the material record of the Shang and Western Chou. But the oracle bone and bronze inscriptions point unmistakably to the existence of Shang specialists capable of using writing to generalize about history and about human affairs, and

17. Li Tsung-t'ung, *History of Ancient Chinese Society* (in Chinese) (Taipei: Huakang, 1954); Chow Ts'e-tsung, "Ancient Chinese *wu* shamanism and its relationship to sacrifices, history, dance-music, and poetry," *Tsing Hua Journal of Chinese Studies*, n.s. 12 (December 1979): 1–59.

18. Tsien, *Written on Bamboo and Silk*, p. 4.

19. T'ang Lan, "A brief discussion on the significance of the collection of bronze vessels of the family of the historiographer of Wei of Western Chou" (in Chinese), *Wenwu* 1978 (3): 19–24.

34. A bronze *tsun*-beaker of the Western Chou
dynasty, found in Shensi. On the right is a
rubbing of the inscription cast on the inside of the
beaker: "Made [this] precious *tsung* vessel for the
honorable father whose day sign is *chi*, for you
children, and you grandchildren. Forever treasure
it and use it for ten thousand years. [Emblem.]"

35. Bronze *p'an*-basin of the Western Chou, cast on behalf of historiographer Ch'iang.

thus invested with the authority to point the way, so to speak, for the benefit of their rulers. That ability was at least partly religious in derivation. It may have come from the original role of the specialists as religious media and from the part that writing played in the communication with ancestral spirits.

6

ACCESS TO THE PATH

Our discussion thus far provides a clear profile of those in ancient China who had great political authority and who wielded its power. They were born into the right clans and (especially) lineages, married the right partners, sat at the central places, were associated with the right myths, behaved in ways deserving popular support, and last but not least had access — at best, exclusive access — to the ancestral wisdom and foresight derived from ritual, art, and writing. All these factors were requisite, of course, but the last was decisive — the determining factor that tipped the balance. The crucial question for aspirants to power in ancient China was: How do I gain access to that access? The answer was: By controlling a few key resources — above all, bronzes — and by amassing the means to control them.

The ancient Chinese themselves made the same statement in the legend of the *chiu ting*, the Nine Bronze Tripods. Texts of the late Chou period or earlier relate how the Great Yü and his son Ch'i, founders of Hsia dynasty, were responsible for the making of the *chiu ting*, which became the symbol of legitimate dynastic rule. These texts deserve to be quoted at some length.

The first reference to the *chiu ting* appears in *Tso Chuan* under the entry for 605 B.C. This was quoted earlier in part, in connection with the meaning of animal motifs in bronze art:

> In the past when the Hsia dynasty was distinguished for its virtue, the distant regions put into pictures their distinctive *wu*, and the nine pastors sent in the metal of their provinces. The *ting*-tripods were cast, with representations on them of those *wu* . . . Hereby a harmony was secured between the high and the low, and all enjoyed the blessings of Heaven. When the virtue of Chieh

95

was all-obscured, the tripods were transferred to Shang, for 600 years. Chòu of Shang proved cruel and oppressive, and they were transferred to Chou. When the virtue is commendable and brilliant, the tripods, though they were small, would be heavy; when it gives place to its reverse, to darkness and disorder, though they were large, they would be light. Heaven blesses intelligent virtue; — on that its favour rests. King Ch'eng fixed the tripods in Chia-ju, and divined that the dynasty should extend through 30 reigns, over 700 years. Though the virtue of Chou is decayed, the decree of Heaven is not yet changed. The weight of the tripods may not yet be inquired about.[1]

In this story it is clear that the *ting*-tripods, the symbols of state, bore images of the animals of all the regions and contained metals from all the regions. The king, thus, not only had access and title to the metal resources but was also in possession of the "means of communication" of the various provinces under his control. These points will be elaborated below.

The other version of the *chiu ting* story comes from *Motse*, the philosophical works of Mo Tzu (c. 468–376 B.C.):

Wu Matse questioned Motse: "Which are wiser, the ghosts and spirits or the sages?" Motse said: "The ghosts and spirits are wiser than the sages by as much as the sharp-eared and keen-sighted surpass the deaf and blind. In ancient times, Emperor Ch'i of Hsia commissioned Fei Lien to dig minerals in mountains and rivers and cast *ting*s at K'un Wu. He ordered Yi to kill the pheasant to invoke the tortoise of Po Jo, saying: 'Let the *ting*s, when completed, be four-legged. Let them be able to cook automatically, without fire, to hide themselves without being lifted, and to move themselves without being carried. So that they may be used for the sacrifice at K'un Wu. May our offering be accepted!' Then the oracle was interpreted as saying: 'I have accepted the offering. Profuse are the white clouds; one to the south, one to the north, one to the west, one to the east. When the nine *ting*s have been completed, they shall be given over to three empires. When the emperor of Hsia loses them the man of Yin will possess them; when the man of Yin loses them the man of Chou will possess them.' Now the transfer from the emperor of Hsia to Yin and Chou took many centuries. Even if the sage planned in counsel with his excellent ministers and superior assistants, could he foresee what would happen after many centuries? Yet the ghosts and spirits can."[2]

This account essentially parallels the other; it, too, focuses on the transfer of power and mentions the procurement of minerals from the mountains and rivers. These stories are the closest things China has to

1. Based on the translation by James Legge, *The Chinese Classics*, vol. 5 (Oxford: Clarendon Press, 1872), p. 293.
2. As translated by Mei Yi-pao, *The Ethical and Political Works of Motse* (London: Probsthain, 1929), pp. 212–213.

myths and legends about the invention of bronze. It would be most interesting to compare them with the Greek myth of the God of Fire, Hephaestus, who made a bronze shield for Achilles (*Iliad*, Book 18).

The *chiu ting* stories are quite straightforward and suggest strongly that the possession of such sacred bronze vessels (Figure 36) served to legitimize the king's rule. These vessels were clear and powerful symbols: they were symbols of wealth because they *were* wealth and possessed the aura of wealth; they were symbols of the all-important ritual that gave their owners access to the ancestors; and they were symbols of the control of metal, which meant control of exclusive access to the ancestors and to political authority.

Wealth and Its Aura

Chiu ting literally means "the nine *ting*-vessels," but the figure nine was commonly used in ancient texts to mean simply a multitude. The ownership and conspicuous display of a multitude of bronze ritual vessels were possible only for the extremely wealthy, and their mass burial with the owner when he or she died must be regarded as conspicuous destruction — almost potlatch-like — as well as a religious act supposedly enabling the dead person to take them along into the afterlife (Figure 37). As archaeologists can gratefully testify, many ancient Chinese graves were extraordinarily rich in furnishings. An outstanding example is the tomb of a royal consort of the Shang dynasty, excavated in 1976 at Yin-hsü, An-yang, Honan province. From this one tomb came the following artifacts:[3]

a wooden chamber and a lacquered wooden coffin
the remains of 16 sacrificial humans and 6 sacrificial dogs
almost 7,000 cowries
more than 200 bronze ritual vessels
5 large bronze bells and 18 small bronze bells
44 bronze implements (27 of them knives)
4 bronze mirrors
1 bronze spatula
more than 130 bronze weapons
4 bronze tigers or tiger heads
more than 20 bronze artifacts of other types
more than 590 jade and jade-like objects
more than 100 jade beads, discs, and fragments
more than 20 opal beads
2 quartz crystal objects

3. "The excavation of Tomb. No. Five at Yin-hsü, An-yang" (in Chinese), *K'ao-ku Hsüeh-pao* 1977 (2): 57–98.

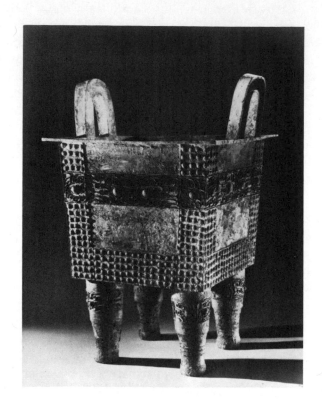

36. A bronze square cauldron excavated outside the Shang city wall at Cheng-chou, Honan, possibly part of a *chiu-ting*-like state treasure.

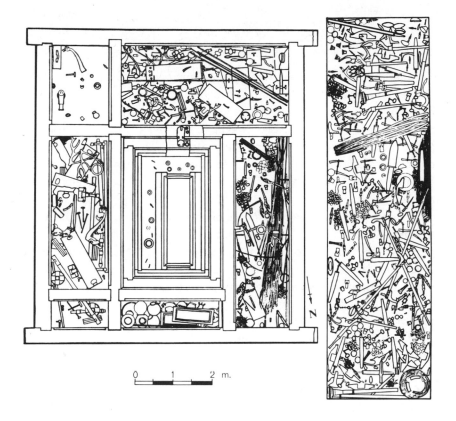

37. Example of a richly furnished grave of a
member of the nobility of ancient China. This
wooden-chambered tomb was excavated recently
at a Ch'u-civilization cemetery in Chiang-ling,
Hupei.

5 bone implements
more than 70 stone sculptures and other stone objects
more than 20 bone arrowheads
more than 490 bone hairpins
3 ivory carvings
4 pottery vessels and 3 clay whistles.

This list is more impressive than most simply because the tomb is one of the very few Shang tombs found in Yin-hsü that had not been plundered. Some of the large tombs in the Royal Cemetery, further north of the river, originally must have contained even greater riches, although their actual archaeological yields were very meager. That the Shang royalty could dispense with wealth of such proportions must have been one of the points the Shang were trying to make in creating such opulently furnished graves.

The *chiu ting*, then, were symbols of this vast wealth, as stated in *Tso Chuan* (entry for 552 B.C.): "When the powerful have conquered the weak, they use their bounty to make ritual vessels and to cast inscriptions to record the deed, to show to their descendants, to publicize the bright and the virtuous, and to penalize those without rituals." In their own words, the ancient Chinese clearly stated that bronze vessels were symbols of wealth, made and used for the aura they gave to rulers and victors.

Bronze vessels were not the only royal symbols, but they were the primary wealth symbols. The most important of the other symbols were the flag and the ax, as is evident in this account of a speech by King Wu of Chou, on the eve of his decisive victory over the Shang: "The time was the chia-tzu day at daybreak; the king in the morning came to Mu Ye by the suburbs of Shang, and then he made a solemn declaration. The king in [his] left hand wielded the yellow battle-axe; in [his] right hand he held the white oxtail flag and waved it aloft. He said: 'From far away you are, people from the Western regions!'"[4] The symbols are obviously those of power: battle-ax as sanction, and flag as manpower. The *chiu ting*, on the other hand, symbolized power of a very different kind. As Yü Wei-ch'ao and Kao Ming made clear in a brilliant essay, a study of the various types and sizes of the *ting*-tripods produced in the course of the Chou dynasty provides a significant key to the changes in the political hierarchy during the period.[5]

4. As translated by Bernhard Karlgren, *The Book of Documents* (Stockholm: Museum of Far Eastern Antiquities, 1950), p. 29.
5. Yü Wei-ch'ao and Kao Ming, "A study of the system of use of *ting*-tripods during the Chou dynasty" (in Chinese), *Peking University Journal (Philosophy and Social Sciences Section)* 1978 (1): 84–98; 1978 (2): 84–97; 1979 (1): 83–96.

Ritual and Communication

As stated in *Kuo Yü* quoted at the beginning of Chapter 3, shamanistic rituals involved a range of paraphernalia, including vessels for food and drink (Figure 38). These ritual vessels of the Three Dynasties were made of various materials—including, notably, bronze—and included many different types, each having its own name. In a comprehensive study, which is to date the most exhaustive survey of Shang and Chou ritual bronzes,[6] Jung Keng described and discussed in detail the major types. Under "food vessels" he lists twelve types; under "wine vessels" twenty-two types; under "water vessels and miscellaneous containers" fifteen types; and under "musical instruments" eight types. His list includes only bronzes and only types for which he could support his discussion with voluminous textual data. Numerous other types of vessels are known only by name in classical texts; many others were made of stone, pottery, wood, basketry, and lacquer. The great variety and taxonomic complexity of ritual paraphernalia make it obvious that Shang and Chou rituals were extremely complicated affairs in which bronze ritual objects played vital roles. It becomes apparent that the performance of such elaborate and luxurious rituals and the consequent communication with ancestral spirits—essential for the art of governance—*depended on* the bronze vessels, with their animal art, and that their possession was essential to assure the rulers' access to ancestral wisdom. The *chiu ting*, therefore, as a symbol of ritual, was a symbol of rule.

Technology and Control

Wealth consisted of goods other than bronze—jade and cowrie, for example—and ritual objects were made of many other materials. But the technology of bronze manufacture alone necessitated such control of resources and organization of manpower that the significance of bronze in the all-important matter of access was unequaled. This is the reason for a *Bronze* Age—at least in the case of China, where ritual vessels formed such a crucial part of the bronze inventory.

Ancient Chinese bronzes were difficult and expensive to make. The process began with the mining of the ore and proceeded to smelting, transporting, alloying, casting, and finally to finishing. Both this long process and the great variety of final products called for an industrial network available only to people with great political power.

6. Jung Keng, *A Comprehensive Study of Shang and Chou Bronze Ritual Vessels* (in Chinese) (Peking: Harvard-Yenching Institute, 1941).

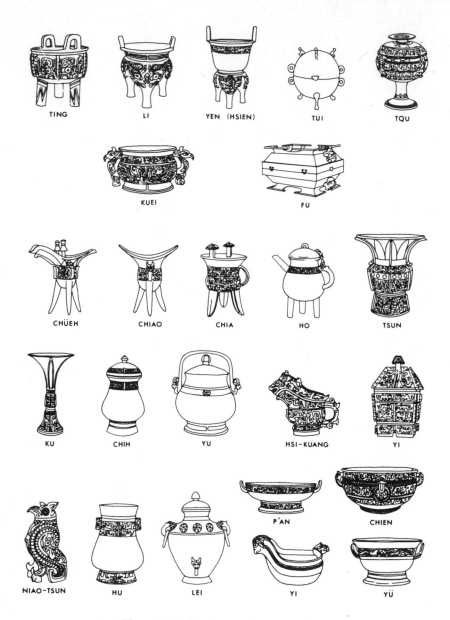

TING LI YEN (HSIEN) TUI TQU

KUEI FU

CHÜEH CHIAO CHIA HO TSUN

KU CHIH YU HSI-KUANG YI

NIAO-TSUN HU LEI P'AN CHIEN YI YÜ

38. The principal varieties of ancient Chinese
bronze ritual vessels for food and drink.

102

Deposits of copper and tin ore had to be located and mined. No ancient Shang mines have yet been found, but a later Chou copper mine was excavated recently at T'ung-lü-shan in Ta-yeh, Hupei, in the middle Yangtze. The mine was more than fifty meters below the surface, reached by vertical shafts, and the slugs scattered around testified to the hundreds of thousands of chunks of ore that had been dug up.[7] In a philosophical treatise of the late Chou, the philosopher-statesman Kuan Tzu (d. 645 B.C.) stated that "of mountains that yield copper there are 467, and of mountains that yield iron there are 3,609." The first-millennium work *Shan Hai Ching* names thirty-four specific mines for iron ore, thirty for copper, 139 for gold, twenty for silver, and five for tin.[8] Very few of these copper and tin mines are included in a recent list of North China mines,[9] but Shih Chang-ju was able to show that numerous copper and tin ore deposits mentioned in the texts of the various historic periods were located within reach of the Shang dynasty capital near An-yang (Figure 39).[10] Presumably these mines were small and were long ago exhausted. A recent account of the Chinese history of metallurgy states that even for ores rich in copper (such as malachite, which was probably the principal copper source in ancient China), three or four hundred kilograms or more of ore were needed for each one hundred kilograms of smelted copper.[11] It may be more realistic to use a one-to-five ratio, considering that some copper ores may have been of inferior quality and that there may have been much waste and inefficiency. From the above-mentioned Shang dynasty tomb excavated in 1976 at Yin-hsü, 468 bronze artifacts were recovered; the excavators have estimated that their total weight was possibly 1,625 kg.[12] Assuming that the tin yield was similar to the copper yield, we can estimate that for the bronzes buried in this one tomb alone more than eight metric tons of ore had to be mined. A late Chou tomb, dated to shortly after 433 B.C. and believed to be that of a marquis of the small state of Tseng, was excavated in 1978 at Lei-ku-tun, Sui Hsien, in eastern Hupei; it has yielded

7. For a concise, popular account of the mine, see Xia Nai and Yin Weizhang, "Digging up an ancient copper mine," *China Reconstructs* 31 (March 1982): 38–40.

8. According to *Ancient Chinese Metallurgy* (in Chinese) (Peking: Wenwu, 1978), p. 31.

9. Wong Wen-hao, *The Mineral Resources of China* (in Chinese), Memoirs of the Geological Survey of China, ser. B, no. 1 (Peking, 1919). For tin, see pp. 103–119; for copper, pp. 119–138.

10. Shih Chang-ju, "Bronze casting techniques of the Yin dynasty" (in Chinese), *Bulletin of the Institute of History and Philology, Academia Sinica* 26 (June 1955): 95–129.

11. *Ancient Chinese Metallurgy*, p. 31.

12. *Tomb No. Five of Yin Hsü* (in Chinese) (Peking: Wenwu, 1980) p. 15.

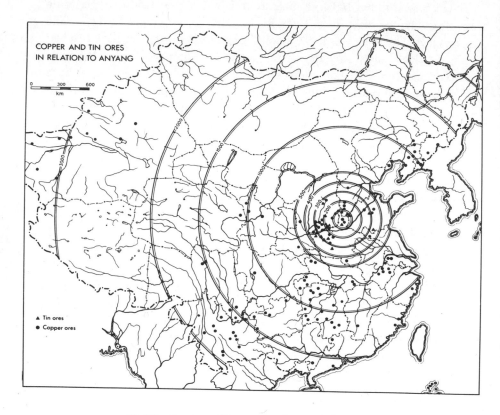

COPPER AND TIN ORES
IN RELATION TO ANYANG

0   300   600
km

▲ Tin ores
● Copper ores

39. Distribution of known and recorded copper
and tin ore deposits in relation to the Shang
dynasty capital near An-yang, according to Shih
Chang-ju.

104

140 bronze containers, 65 bronze bells, and over 4,500 bronze weapons.[13] The weight of every object has not been given in the preliminary reports, but many of the ritual vessels and bells are unusually large; two containers weigh 320 kg. and 362 kg., respectively, and the largest bell is 204 kg. A very rough calculation results in a minimum of 10,000 kg. of bronze products, or 100 metric tons of ore, for this one tomb of a single nobleman. It is hardly surprising that ancient mines should long ago have been exhausted. The search for copper and tin ore and the protection of the mines must have required the mobilization of considerable forces, and could have been one of the factors prompting the frequent movement of the Hsia and the Shang royal capitals. (Historical texts record nine capitals for Hsia and thirteen for Shang.) Ores were smelted at the mines and probably molded into ingots for easy transportation back to the foundries; the transport routes were doubtless frequented by armed convoys.

At the foundries the ingots were melted and cast into artifacts through a delicate "piece-mold" process (Figure 40). The successive steps of the casting process have been described by Wan Chia-pao:

1. A model was first made. The pattern was incised partly on the model and partly, later, on the mold, according to the nature of the pattern. The model was then baked.

2. To form the mold, a layer of clay about fifteen millimeters thick was applied to the model. The edges of the mold were finished with a knife, and some kind of release agent was applied to prevent the model from adhering to the mold. The divisions of the mold and the number of pieces were all determined by the shape of the object. The mold was then baked.

3. The "core" was made by scraping down the surface of the model. The thickness of clay scraped away was equal to, or a little thicker than, the wall of the bronze object to be cast.

4. The pieces of the mold were assembled around the core and the whole was bound with grass rope and/or put into a sand box to ensure rigidity. The molds were assembled upside down, as evidenced by the use of chaplets to support the suspended core of the ring foot, or pedestal.

5. Finally, the molten bronze was poured into the mold. There is no evidence to show to what temperature the mold was heated before the

13. *The Tomb of Marquis Yi of Tseng in Sui Hsien* (in Chinese) (Wu-han: Hupei Provincial Museum, 1979); *The Tomb of Marquis Yi of Tseng in Sui Hsien* (Peking: Wen-wu, 1980).

bronze was poured; but it must have been very high to avoid sudden cooling of the molten bronze on contact with the mold. The clear patterns on Shang bronzes reveal that no such loss of fluidity took place during this critical step of the casting process.[14]

The piece-mold process, most scholars agree,[15] was distinctively Chinese and in all likelihood developed indigeneously. When large and intricately decorated vessels were cast using this technique, large-scale cooperation within the shop, perfect timing, and shop specialization were all absolutely necessary. Again, possession of bronzes of this kind was a forceful symbol of power; in fact, with its complex technology, bronze may have been a major cause of the characteristic power politics of ancient China.

14. Li Chi and Wan Chia-pao, *Studies of the Bronze-ku Beaker* (in Chinese) (Taipei: Institute of History and Philology, Academia Sinica, 1964), pp. 121–122.

15. Noel Barnard, *Bronze Casting and Bronze Alloys in Ancient China*, Monumenta Serica Monograph 14 (Tokyo, 1961); Noel Barnard and Satō Tamotsu, *Metallurgical Remains of Ancient China* (Tokyo: Nichiosha, 1975); Wilma Fairbank, "Piece-mold craftsmanship and Shang bronze design," *Archives of the Chinese Art Society of America* 16 (1962): 8–15; Ursula Franklin, "On bronze and other metals in early China," in *The Origin of Chinese Civilization*, ed. David N. Keightley (Berkeley: University of California Press, 1983).

7

THE RISE OF POLITICAL AUTHORITY

Having described the various factors that enabled political power to be concentrated in the hands of a ruling elite, we will here examine the historical evidence and see how these factors may have come about in the course of time. Briefly, the factors are as follows:

1. Individual status within a kinship system of agnatic clans and segmentary lineages, organized hierarchically
2. A network of interactive regional polities, each in control of significant resources and together forming interlocked and mutually reinforcing systems
3. Military apparatus, including bronze weapons and chariots
4. Meritorious deeds (of a nature beneficial to the populace), both mythologically inherent in, and actually embodied by, living rulers
5. Writing as a vehicle of information pertaining to one's position in the kinship system and to spiritual (ancestral) wisdom, the key to governance and to predictive power
6. Exclusive access to heaven and heavenly spirits through means other than writing, such as shamanistic rituals (with their music and dance) together with animal art and bronze paraphernalia
7. Wealth and its aura.

All of these factors were, of course, causally interrelated, and their significance in the ancient Chinese context is unquestionable and empirically established. When they are viewed in isolation, however, their hierarchy in terms of their causal dynamics is obscure. To determine how such a power system began in ancient China, we have to go back to China's prehistory — prior to the Three Dynasties. Such an effort must be undertaken within a framework of cultural prehistory, in which there was, in North China, a succession of cultures (P'ei-li-kang, 7000–5000 B.C.; Yang-shao, 5000–3000 B.C.; and Lung-shan, 3000–2200 B.C.). But

107

the usual characterization of these cultures in terms of pottery types and styles is inadequate for our effort to trace the rise of political authority. We must examine the specific archaeological manifestations of these "enabling factors" before any effort can be made to trace their archaeological history. The following kinds of archaeological evidence will suit our task specifically and empirically.

1. The specific uses to which bronze and other copper alloys were put provide important clues to the areas of culture where technological innovation and concentration of resources were important. The use of these alloys for agricultural implements would indicate that technology was important for the production and accumulation of wealth. Such use, however, has not been widely found in ancient China. "Throughout China archaeologists have excavated many Shang and Chou dynasty sites, from which a large number of agricultural implements have been brought to light; but agricultural implements of bronze are rare — this is an undeniable objective fact."[1] While agricultural implements continued to be made of stone, wood, antler, and bone during the Bronze Age (Figure 41), bronze was used conspicuously for the manufacturing of weapons, ritual paraphernalia (food vessels, wine vessels, and musical instruments), some ornaments, and such carpenter's tools as the ax, adz, and chisel. The carpenter's tools were presumably necessary for the construction of wooden chariots, which were the most formidable weapon of the Bronze Age. This pattern of use is highly distinctive of the Chinese Bronze Age, in which bronze was associated primarily with ritual and with war, "the two principal affairs of the state" (*Tso Chuan*, entry for 579 B.C.). In other words, if bronze epitomized the way in which scarce resources were used in ancient China, then political culture played a central role in Chinese civilization at its very inception.

2. The archaeological study of settlement patterns provides fundamental information on the hierarchical interrelationship of contemporaneous sites over vast areas. The hierarchical levels can be determined by the size of the settlements and the nature of their remains. At the same time, it must be emphasized that spatial configuration alone is no reliable guide to settlement relationships, and that where textual information is available it should be used.[2] For ancient China, unfortunately, regional

1. Ch'en Wen-hua, "A tentative discussion on several issues in the history of agricultural implements in China" (in Chinese), *Kao-ku Hsüeh-pao* 1981 (4): 410.
2. One example of such studies is K. C. Chang, "Settlement patterns in Chinese archaeology: A case study from the Bronze Age," in *Prehistoric Settlement Pattern Studies: Retrospect and Prospect*, ed. E. Z. Vogt, Jr., and R. Levanthal (Albuquerque: University of New Mexico Press, 1983).

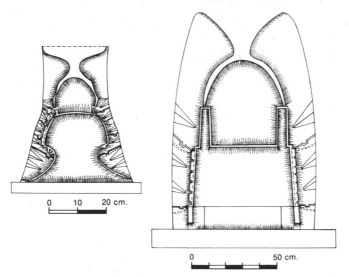

40. Clay piece-molds for casting bronze vessels, dating from the Shang dynasty. The V-shaped incisions on the sides of the molds provided room for expansion when the mold was heated by the molten metal. After use, piece-molds could be taken apart without damage, but the core usually had to be broken up.

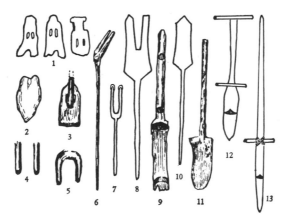

41. Some agricultural implements from ancient China: *lei* (4–8, 13), *ssu* (1–3, 10, 12), and *ch'iu* (9, 11). Most were made of wood, but number 1 was of bone and 2 was lithic. 1–4 are Neolithic; 5 is Shang; 6–10 are Han; 11 was Eastern Chou; 12 and 13 are from present-day Tibet.

surveys are not routine archaeological operations, and ancient cities are studied more or less one at a time. As a consequence, there is a dearth of data on settlement patterns in the Chinese Bronze Age, and in this respect we rely mainly upon textual data.

3. In archaeology there are standard ways of recognizing differences in social status by looking at architectural and mortuary practices. In the architecture of the Three Dynasties, there was first of all a division between above-ground buildings (with pounded-earth floors or foundation platforms) and underground buildings. Considering the amount of labor that went into above-ground buildings, it is likely that they belonged to the elite. They may have been "palaces," "dwellings," or various combinations of these (Figure 42); but no clear-cut distinctions can be made at most, if not all, archaeological sites because very little remains of the contents of these buildings.

Regarding mortuary remains, there is first of all a division between large graves with wooden chambers and small graves without wooden chambers. The former — including several categories according to shape, structure, and number of ramps — required massive amounts of labor to construct and often contain sacrificial human victims. As a rule, the large graves were richly furnished, perhaps both to assure the departed a luxurious afterlife and to display conspicuously the master's wealth. The smaller graves, on the other hand, were those of members of the lower classes, again divided into several groups according to the condition of the burial and the amount of furnishings. Graves of certain sizes and degrees of opulence were also sometimes grouped according to particular plans, throwing light on patterns of social and political grouping.

4. Evidence of institutionalized violence usually means that war was a social fixture, and that violence was not, in general, merely an individual or occasional act. A scalped skull or an arrowhead embedded in human remains does not necessarily mean institutionalization of violence; but when such skulls and remains are found in conjunction with weapons in graves, or with defensive city ramparts or chariots, they do indicate this. Arrowhead factories or remains of soldiers buried in formation imply that war was a state affair, as does the use of scarce metals for weaponry rather than for productive technology.

The material means of access that we have discussed provide obvious archaeological evidence of the system of political authority. Oracle bones suggest shamanistic communication, but the inscriptions found on them are acts that are more political than religious. The animal motifs on

42. Reconstructions of ancient Chinese "palaces."
Upper: Hsia dynasty palace excavated at
Erh-li-t'ou. Lower: Shang dynasty palace at P'an-
lung-ch'eng site in Huang-p'i, Hupei.

animal motifs

ritual objects point to shamanism, but their use on luxurious and scarce art objects spells shamanistic politics.

Using the above as sensitive indicators of the system of politics that characterized the Three Dynasties, we can take a good look at the prehistoric data and see how such a system emerged.

For the P'ei-li-kang and Yang-shao periods, from the beginning of agricultural life in the Yellow River valley to the height of development of village farming, we can simply say that according to the archaeological record, a system of political authority with the distinctive features mentioned above did not exist. There is no evidence of marked social or political divisions, or of institutionalized violence. For the Yang-shao Culture of Shensi, however, three notable items deserve discussion.

The first point has to do with the layout of some of the Yang-shao villages, such as those near Pan-p'o (Figure 43) and Chiang-chai, both near Sian, where houses appear in clusters forming segments of the village, and where the clusters make a rough circle around a central plaza.[3] According to a cross-cultural study of village layouts and social composition,[4] such a "planned," segmented village layout strongly suggests that the houses sheltered members of unilinear kin groups. Clans and lineages characteristic of Three Dynasties society may have had their beginning in the Yang-shao period, if not before.

Second, the possible existence of clans and lineages during the Yang-shao period is strengthened by the fact that there are potters' marks on many pottery vessels of the Yang-shao Culture at many sites, including both Pan-p'o and Chiang-chai. A number of scholars contend that these marks are the earliest examples of Chinese writing. To be sure, some of these marks are identical to certain characters in the Shang and Chou writing systems and could have been the source from which the latter were derived. But these marks occur singly, providing no evidence for a written language. They are better viewed as clan and lineage emblems, like many Shang and Chou characters cast on ritual bronze vessels.

3. For Pan-p'o, see *Hsi-an Pan-p'o* (Peking: Wenwu, 1962), p. 9; and Shih Hsing-pang, *Clan Community at Pan-p'o* (in Chinese) (Sian: Shensi Jen-min, 1979), p. 6. For Chiang-chai, see "Outline of the fourth to the eleventh seasons of excavations at the site of Chiang-chai, in Lin-t'ung" (in Chinese), *K'ao-ku yü Wen-wu* 1980 (3): 1–13; and Kung Ch'i-ming and Yen Wen-ming, "Social organization and structure of the inhabitants of the early settlement at Chiang-chai according to its layout" (in Chinese), *K'ao-ku yü Wen-wu* 1981 (1): 63–71.

4. K. C. Chang, "Study of the neolithic social grouping: Examples from the New World," *American Anthropologist* 60 (April 1958): 298–334.

43. A model showing the layout of the Yang-shao
Neolithic village at Pan-p'o, Sian, Shensi.

These Yang-shao vessels were apparently utilitarian, not ritual vessels, and the emblems—if that is what they were—tell us more about the nature of the society than they do about the communicative role of writing, such as that which later linked the living and the ancestral worlds.

The third item pertains to the presence of shamans in the Yang-shao Culture. From *Shan Hai Ching*, the first-millennium B.C. "book of shamanism,"[5] we learn about a number of shaman-like characters who wore snakes or dragons on their ears, hands, and ankles. Pottery basins found at Pan-p'o display a recurrent decorative motif painted in black or dark brown on a red surface: a human face with a fish design at each ear (Figure 44). Marilyn Fu has suggested that these faces might be those of shamans and that the wearing of fishes might be compared with the wearing of snakes by the shamans described in *Shan Hai Ching*. If so, later Chinese shamanism may date back to the Yang-shao, if not earlier, although as yet we have no evidence to connect shamanism with the kind of political system that was present in the Three Dynasties.

Such a connection, however, does appear in the archaeological finds of the subsequent phases of prehistory. I refer to the cultures of these phases as Lungshanoid, but in different regions we can speak of specific regional cultures such as the Lung-shan Culture of Honan, the Ta-wen-k'ou Culture of Shantung, the Ch'ü-chia-ling Culture of Hupei, and the Liang-chu Culture of Chekiang.[6] These cultures sprang up in various areas of China at roughly the same time—late fourth and early third millennium B.C.—and they have yielded a long and rich series of archaeological evidence pertaining to ancient Chinese political culture.

Scapulimancy—divination by heating the shoulder blades of animals—became widespread throughout North China during this period, but turtle shells were not yet used for this purpose and oracle bones were not inscribed.

The use of *potters' marks* continued, but there is as yet no firm evidence of a written language in this period.

A number of *small metal objects* have been found at Lung-shan sites in Shantung and at some contemporary sites elsewhere, but no metal was used for either ritual vessels or weapons.

There is some *evidence of warfare*: one or two Lung-shan Culture

5. Yuan Hsing-p'ei, "A preliminary exploration of the *Shan Hai Ching*" (in Chinese), *Chung-hua Wen-shih Lun-ts'ung*, September 1979 (3): 7–35.

6. K. C. Chang, *The Archaeology of Ancient China* (New Haven: Yale University Press, 1977), ch. 4.

44. Human face with fish designs at the ears,
painted on the inside of a pottery bowl of the
Yang-shao Culture at Pan-p'o.

villages in North China had rammed-earth walls and at one Lung-shan site in Han-tan, Hopei province, there is evidence of a village raid, including skeletons of bodies that had been thrown into a well and skulls that give indications of having been scalped (Figure 45). But it has not yet been firmly established that these sites date from a period prior to the Three Dynasties.

At some Yangtze valley Lungshanoid sites there are *pottery vessels and ritual objects* (long, square tubes) bearing animal masks similar to the *t'ao-t'ieh* masks found on bronze vessels of later periods. These finds might possibly indicate that here, too, animal agents functioned as bridges between the living and the dead in shamanistic rituals.

Sophisticated *wheel-made pottery*, characterized by intricate workmanship, eggshell-thin walls, and a polished black exterior, made a conspicuous appearance during this period. There is no question that these pottery vessels were made by specialized craftsmen and for ritual purposes.

At a number of Lung-shan sites in Honan, *clay phalli* have been found (Figure 46). These have been used — rightly, I believe — to demonstrate the existence of male ancestor worship at this time.

Large, wooden-chambered, and extremely well-furnished tombs are common in the Ta-wen-k'ou Culture of Shantung and northern Kiangsu (Figure 47). On the basis of a thorough analysis of a number of Neolithic burial sites in eastern coastal China, Richard Pearson concludes that "the sequence of burial sites in the Chinese coastal Neolithic, leading to Dawenkou [Ta-wen-k'ou], shows increasing wealth and social differentiation and a decline in the status of women and children . . . The society was gradually changing to one in which males appear to have had power and wealth, and craft specialization was beginning to emerge. Some spatial segregation of burials, into groups of men, women, and children together, suggests the increasing importance of lineage."[7]

All of the above, taken together, are archaeological manifestations of a political culture that did not yet have all the characteristics of the Three Dynasties, but that did indeed appear to provide a foundation for the latter. The society was sharply ranked — on the basis of an agnatic lineage system, at least in large part — and was characterized by violence; ceremonies featuring ritual paraphernalia, animal agents, and animal bones for divination; and conspicuous display of wealth. Moreover, evidence for such a society appears on the scene more or less simulta-

7. Richard Pearson, "Social complexity in Chinese coastal neolithic sites," *Science* 213 (September 1981): 1086.

45. Upper: Human skeletons found at the bottom of a well at a Lung-shan Culture site in Han-tan, Hopei, excavated in the 1950s. Lower: Human skulls from the same site, showing evidence of scalping.

46. Clay phallus models from Lung-shan Culture sites in Honan. Height is approximately 12 centimeters.

47. A richly furnished grave at the Neolithic site at Ta-wen-k'ou, T'ai-an, Shantung. Photograph at top shows the pit of Tomb 10; drawing at bottom shows artifacts recovered from the grave.

neously in several geographic regions that are contiguous but that encompass widely divergent natural habitats. On the other hand, in none of these cultures is there evidence of significant advances in productive technology, or strong indication of interregional competition for land or resources.

The period of the Lungshanoid cultures, dated to the third millennium B.C., directly preceded the Three Dynasties and thus coincided with the period of the heroes and sages of later Chinese legendary history. At one time, historians believed that the entire legendary period had been fabricated by Han dynasty philosophers. In recent years, as the result of archaeological — particularly textual — discoveries, we have become increasingly confident of the essential authenticity of the ancient texts, and of the historicity of the many legends. The legends of the ancient tribal chiefs, heroes, and sages may thus provide useful clues to our reading of the Lungshanoid archaeological record.

The portrait of the political culture that emerges from these legends is extremely persuasive.[8] Different areas of China are depicted as having been occupied by members of various clans, such as the Chi clan of the Yellow Emperor (the clan from which the Chou ultimately derived); the Tzu and Ssu clans; the Ying clan of the Huai River valley; the Feng clan of Shantung; the Six Clans of Chu-jung in the central Yangtze valley; and many other clans of various sizes and degrees of importance. Tribes were organized on the basis of clan membership and affiliation. Different tribes had distinctive subcultures (Figure 48). It is tempting to identify some of the regional Lungshanoid cultures with some of the legendary tribal groups. No definitive identification is possible until written records are found and enable the cultures to be identified, but thus far archaeological evidence does not contradict the legendary picture.

The legends also provide information on the rules governing political succession — in particular, those pertaining to the so-called *shan jang*, or "succession by invitation," instituted by the emperors Yao and Shun. When Yao was emperor he selected Shun, a widely admired and virtuous man, to be his successor rather than Tan-chu, Yao's own son; and when it came time for Shun to select his heir he chose the Great Yü, rather than his own son Shang-chün, because Yü had proved his merit by controlling the flood. These acts were cited by classical philosophers as exemplary

8. Two examples of outstanding scholarship on the legendary prehistory of the Chinese are Hsü hsü-sheng, *The Legendary Period of the Ancient History of China* (in Chinese), rev.ed. (Peking: Science Press, 1960); and Fu Ssu-nien, *Collection of the Scholarly Writings of Mr. Fu Ssu-nien* (in Chinese) (Hong Kong: Lung-men, 1969).

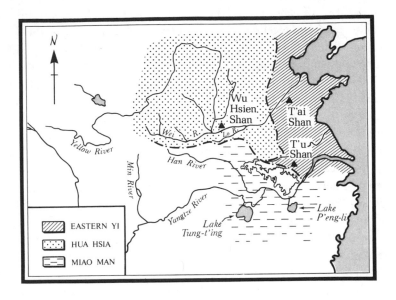

48. Map of the three major ethnic groups of
ancient China, according to the classification of
Hsü Hsü-sheng.

behavior which in part gave the rulers their moral authority. But the legends could also be vestiges of an ancient system of rotary succession to high office, a system I have reconstructed for the Shang kingship.[9]

Archaeology and legendary history meet at the beginning of the Three Dynasties. The Hsia can be only tentatively identified with the Erh-li-t'ou Culture, as mentioned earlier, but evidence from the Shang and Chou has essentially confirmed the broad outline and many details of the textual history. There is now no longer any question about the political culture of the Three Dynasties: in the Erh-li-t'ou Culture we find all of its essential archaeological manifestations, except writing (Figure 49).

Now that we have reviewed the archaeological record pertaining to the rise of political authority in ancient China, what can we say of the process that underlies the history? Let us turn again to the earlier parts of the Neolithic. Several thousand years before the Christian era, the Chinese landscape was already dotted with farming villages whose inhabitants were grouped into clans and lineages. Membership in these groups was important enough to be, apparently, the sole reason for the first use of written symbols in that part of the world. (In other parts of the world, the first use of written symbols was often for other purposes — for example, economic transactions.) The ranking of members within each of these villages was presumably based on kinship relations. This archaic state of affairs was the baseline of ancient Chinese society, and subsequent progress consisted essentially in hierarchically rearranging the relationships among the villages — a process that probably began during the Lungshanoid period.

The rearrangement was accomplished via two specific processes that worked toward the same result from opposite directions. First, there was the fission of villages and the segmentation of the lineages, which resulted in an increase in the number of individual villages. Second, there was the political subjugation of some villages by others, which resulted in a decrease in the number of independent political units. The combined result was increasing stratification in terms of political authority, both within and among the villages. At the higher end of the spectrum were people nearest the main line of lineage descent in the conquering villages; at the opposite end were people farthest away from the main lineage and people from vanquished villages.

This was not a stable system of political authority. There were many

9. K. C. Chang, "T'ien Kan: A key to the history of Shang," in *Ancient China: Studies in Early Civilization*, ed. D. Roy and T. H. Tsien (Hong Kong: Chinese University of Hong Kong Press, 1978).

0   5 cm.

49. A bronze *chüeh*-cup excavated from the Hsia dynasty site at Erh-li-t'ou, near Lo-yang, Honan. This is one of the five earliest bronze ritual vessels that have so far been brought to light in China.

clans and lineages, and their numbers constantly increased by fission. Eventually there were so many that maintaining the relative political status of different villages, clans, and collateral lineages could not be accomplished by genealogy alone but required practical means. Of these, there were mainly three: moral authority (the carrot); coercive force (the stick); and exclusive wisdom derived from exclusive access to the spiritual world (religion and ceremonialism). By the Three Dynasties period, the shape of the ancient Chinese political system had become clear and distinctive. A small number of states were born in the several regions of China.

What we call civilization was both a result of and a requisite for this rise of political authority. Civilization is the manifestation of concentrated wealth. In ancient China, wealth was procured primarily through political power and was, as well, a necessary condition for the acquisition and maintenance of that power. Rulers could wield political power only by first establishing political authority; and, as we have seen, the several factors that enabled rulers to establish such authority manifest themselves archaeologically as components of the civilization.

In this equation it is difficult, but not impossible, to single out the causes of change. First, let us clarify our terms. In the literature on the ancient world, we frequently encounter the words "civilization," "urbanism," and "state." In the Chinese case, it is clear that all three are aspects of the same equation. As villages became larger and more complex, they turned into urban centers or urban networks. As they assumed new hierarchical arrangements, they organized into political units, some of which we call states. Civilization (to repeat) is the manifestation of material wealth in concentrated form, which is both a result of and a requisite for political authority. In our equation, then, we can eliminate technology per se as the primary motive force for the emergence of either civilization or state, because in China the initial concentration of resources (civilization) was accomplished by political means (the state society), and not by advanced technology — as we have seen from our study of ancient bronzes. We can also eliminate population pressure and geographic restriction as two primary causes, either singly or in concert, since China provided ample room for expansion. The formation of several parallel states adjacent to one another may have resulted in political barriers to expansion; but historical data from the Chou show that political expansion could be accomplished by establishing new towns in distant uninhabited lands, well beyond the state's borders.

What we do see in the Chinese picture is the primacy of the political culture in the distribution of resources. When population increased and more mouths had to be fed, groups were sent off to found new settlements, which were given support and protection by their parental polities under a system of hierarchical power and resource distribution. When settlements of different political stripes came into contact and conflict, conquest and subjugation again resulted in hierarchical systems with numerous components. Power and wealth were mutually dependent, fostering both themselves and each other. Over time, we see increasing numbers, increasing volumes, and increasing complexity. Between beginning and climax is a continuum of increasing complexity, and we are free to cut the continuum into segments and devise our schemes of societal evolution.

With the above discussion as a base, we are in a position to take a brief look at some of the theories pertaining to ancient civilizations in general, and to ancient Chinese civilization in particular. We might well be curious to know if and in what way the conclusions we have reached thus far confirm or contradict some of the other theories pertaining to ancient China and its politics. Naturally we are concerned here only with Western theories, not with the traditional Confucian theory, which is in itself a part of our data base.

Western theories on ancient Chinese politics center on the concept of the Oriental society. "The concept of Oriental society as a distinct type arose at the end of the 18th century and was a contribution of the so-called classical economists. It was created because these economists could not comprehend the economics of ancient Egypt and Mesopotamia, or contemporary China and India, on the basis of their understanding of Greece and Rome or of Europe under feudalism or capitalism. Treated by Marx, the idea passed to the sociologist Max Weber, then to [Karl Wittfogel] who has given the theory its most extensive treatment."[10] It would be very interesting to look at this concept and its changing history in the light of what we now know about the inception of Chinese society. Unfortunately, neither Marx nor Weber nor Wittfogel had access to archaeological data from the Three Dynasties, and both their characterization of Oriental society and their speculations about the causes of its formation were based upon extrapolation from later histories, often known to them only second-hand.

10. Morton H. Fried, *Readings in Cultural Anthropology*, vol. 2 (New York: T. Y. Crowell, 1959), p. 95.

According to the historical paradigm of Marx, among the three or four alternative routes out of the primitive communal system was the Oriental system.

> The fundamental characteristic of this system was the self-sustaining unit of manufacture and agriculture within the village commune, which thus contains all the conditions for reproduction and surplus production within itself, and which therefore resisted disintegration and economic evolution more stubbornly than any other system. The theoretical absence of property in oriental despotism thus masks the tribal or communal property which is its base. Such systems may be decentralised or centralised, more despotic or more democratic in form, and variously organised. Where such small community-units exist as part of a larger unity, they may devote part of their surplus product to pay the costs of the (larger) community, i.e., for war, religious worship, etc., and for economically necessary operations such as irrigation and the maintenance of communications, which will thus appear to be done by the higher community, the despotic government suspended above the small communities . . . The "closed" nature of the communal units means that cities hardly belong into the economy at all, arising only where the location is particularly favourable to external trade, or where the ruler and his satraps exchange their revenue (surplus product) for labour, which they expend as a labour fund. The Asiatic system is therefore not yet a class society, or if it is a class society, then it is the most primitive form.[11]

The sociological literature generated by the scanty writings of Marx on the Oriental (or Asiatic) system is enormous,[12] but to what extent ancient China — which has always been considered to fit this paradigm — figured in the formulation of the scheme is a legitimate question. The European literature on Chinese history that was available to Marx was obviously limited in scope and insight.[13] In fact, Perry Anderson flatly stated that "Marx's comments on China furnish . . . a final illustration of the limits of his comprehension of Asian history."[14] Be that as it may, Marx's formulation of a system of static, self-contained village communities does not in any way conform with our current picture of ancient Chinese towns and cities, viewed as being in dynamic interaction within a constantly shifting, hierarchical economic and political system.

In contrast to Marx's inadequacies, Max Weber's access to Chinese historiography and his contribution to it are almost worthy of a

---

11. Karl Marx, *Pre-Capitalist Economic Formations*, introd. by E. J. Hobsbawm (New York: International Publishers, 1965), pp. 33–34.
12. See Perry Anderson, *Lineages of the Absolutist State* (London: NLB, 1974), pp. 462ff., under the heading "The Asiatic Mode of Production."
13. Marx, *Pre-Capitalist Economic Formations*, pp. 21–22.
14. Anderson, *Lineages of the Absolutist State*, p. 492.

sinologist.[15] His conception of the "patrimonial state" is, of course, not confined to the Chinese or even the Oriental system. Such states (where "the prince organizes his political power over extrapatrimonial areas and political subjects — which is not discretionary and not enforced by physical coercion — just like the exercise of his patriarchal power"), or at least "a fairly strong patrimonial character," are found "in the majority of all great continental empires until and even after the beginning of modern times."[16] In his application of the concept of the patrimonial state to China, Weber gives the following characterization:

> Here too the power of patrimonial officialdom was based on river regulation, especially canal construction . . . and on tremendous military fortifications; again these were only possible through intensive use of compulsory labor and through the use of magazines for storing payments in kind, from which the officials drew their benefices and the army its equipment and provisions. In addition, the patrimonial bureaucracy benefitted from the even more complete absence of a landed nobility than was the case in Egypt . . . In the main, patrimonial officialdom was confronted only by the sibs [clans] as autochthanous power, aside from merchant and craft guilds as they are found everywhere.[17]

In its essential features the patrimonial state does resemble the Shang case, as pointed out by Paul Wheatley.[18] But as van der Sprenkel observed,[19] Weber made use of historical materials taken from widely different periods of Chinese history. Whereas the confrontation between the central patrimonial bureaucracy and the local gentry based on exogamous clans may have been a significant occurrence in later historical China, in the Three Dynasties period the patrimonial state itself was based on an exogamous clan, which was in constant interaction with other clans. Furthermore, the patrimony may have provided an institutional framework for the state, but the state power was based on kinship only fictitiously; it had to manifest and exert itself through the various practical means mentioned above. Therefore, to call Shang and the other ancient Chinese states "patrimonial" does not immediately identify the key mechanisms of the political system involved in the formation of the state. We must also discover the real bases of political power.

Weber's emphasis on river regulation (rivers were, in his view, used

15. Otto B. van der Sprenkel, "Max Weber on China," in *Studies in the Philosophy of History*, ed. George Nadel (New York: Harper & Row, 1965).

16. Max Weber, *Economy and Society: An Outline of Interpretive Sociology*, vol. 2 (Berkeley: University of California Press, 1978), p. 1013.

17. Weber, *Economy and Society*, p. 1047.

18. Paul Wheatley, *The Pivot of Four Quarters* (Chicago: Aldine, 1971), p. 99.

19. Van der Sprenkel, "Max Weber on China," p. 199.

Art, Myth, and Ritual

mainly for transportation) as a principal power base has been developed much further by Wittfogel in his theory of "hydraulic societies," or irrigation civilizations.[20] Without going into the details of that theory, I will simply say that the theory of water control as the primary base of state power does not find support in the archaeology of the Three Dynasties. Evidence for water control is not prominent in the archaeological or inscriptional record of ancient China; the mechanisms of power evolved in other realms.

Clearly, our discussion here will be highly pertinent in evaluating any historiographic and sociological generalizations about China. It is even possible that some day, generalizations about such issues as the dynamics of the first emergence of civilization on earth could be devised from the data dealt with here. Theories of history have typically been built on the history of Western civilization. In the modern world, Western civilization has undergone the most remarkable expansion in the annals of mankind, quickly enveloping the globe, and it has brought with it theories formulated on the basis of its own formidable and massive history to explain the origin and history of all human society. Since these theories occasionally guided social and political activists in their endeavors to change the world, they are of more than academic interest.

It is time to consider the possibility that theories of history could be built on the development of other civilizations and that such theories could offer new insights, not only relating to abstract principles about the past but also to political action in the future. China itself is one reason why such a reconsideration is so timely.

Chinese history is as formidable and massive as Western history, but it has not been analyzed in the same way to generate universal laws.[21] When China and the West encountered each other in the nineteenth and early twentieth centuries, there was essentially a one-way flow of sociological theory from West to East.[22] At that time, most Western social theorists and historiographers did not have the tools or skills to

20. Karl Wittfogel, *Oriental Despotism: A Comparative Study of Total Power* (New Haven: Yale University Press, 1957); idem, "The theory of Oriental society," in *Readings in Anthropology*, ed. M. H. Fried, vol. 2 (New York: T. Y. Crowell, 1959), pp. 94–113.
21. On generalizations in Chinese historiography, see Arthur F. Wright, "On the uses of generalizations in the study of Chinese history," in *Generalization in the Writing of History*, ed. Louis Gottschalk (Chicago: University of Chicago Press, 1963), pp. 36–58.
22. Donald W. Treadgold, *The West in Russia and China*, vol. 2, *China: 1582–1949* (Cambridge: Cambridge University Press, 1973), deals with the impact of Western thought on China from the arrival of the Jesuits at the end of the Ming dynasty to the contemporary period.

128

study unfamiliar Chinese history through its more than twenty centuries of written records. Nor were many of them inclined to fully digest the Chinese data with a view to extracting new generalizations. Our brief digressions on Marx and Weber illustrate this point. In recent years, social science paradigms, models, generalizations, and constructs of many kinds have been applied to China, but original research based on primary Chinese sources has been so lacking that Mary Wright was once moved to ask, rather plaintively, "But if the aims of social scientists are to establish the broadest generalizations obtainable, and if the breadth of any generalization depends on the range of phenomena to which it applied, do the intellectual demands of their own research not lead them to the study of the appropriate portions of the Chinese record?"[23]

This question is of particular pertinence today because in recent years our knowledge of Chinese history has been significantly expanded by archaeology, enabling us for the first time to observe how it all began — "it" being Chinese civilization. In this book, I have made a preliminary effort to account for the rise of political authority in ancient China, with the aim of providing some food for thought in historical theory. The issue of the rise of political authority is one that pertains to every ancient civilization. But it is only now, when new data have become available, that we can seriously begin to explore the question in the light of Chinese facts. The process that emerges from such an exploration might be identical with those that have been hypothesized by Western theorists, on the basis of the history of Western civilization; but it might also be significantly different. Either way, Chinese records will make an important contribution to historical theory: they will confirm it through substantial new data, or they will modify it to some degree, resulting in generalizations of ever wider applicability and validity.

23. Mary Wright, "The social sciences and the Chinese historical record," *Journal of Asian Studies* 20 (February 1961): 220–221.

APPENDIX: The Kings of the Three Dynasties

The Hsia Dynasty

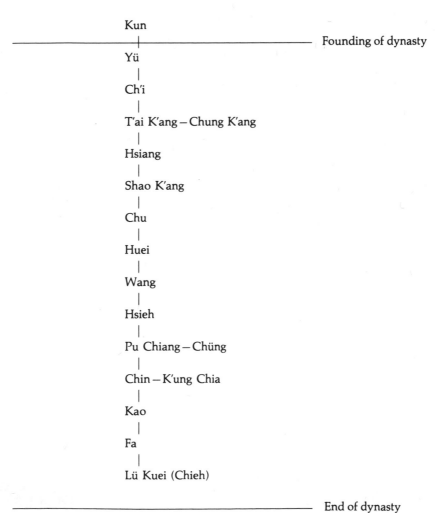

```
                        Kun
──────────────────────────────────────────  Founding of dynasty
                         │
                        Yü
                         │
                        Ch'i
                         │
            T'ai K'ang — Chung K'ang
                         │
                       Hsiang
                         │
                     Shao K'ang
                         │
                        Chu
                         │
                       Huei
                         │
                       Wang
                         │
                       Hsieh
                         │
              Pu Chiang — Chüng
                         │
              Chin — K'ung Chia
                         │
                       Kao
                         │
                        Fa
                         │
               Lü Kuei (Chieh)
```

── End of dynasty

The Shang Dynasty

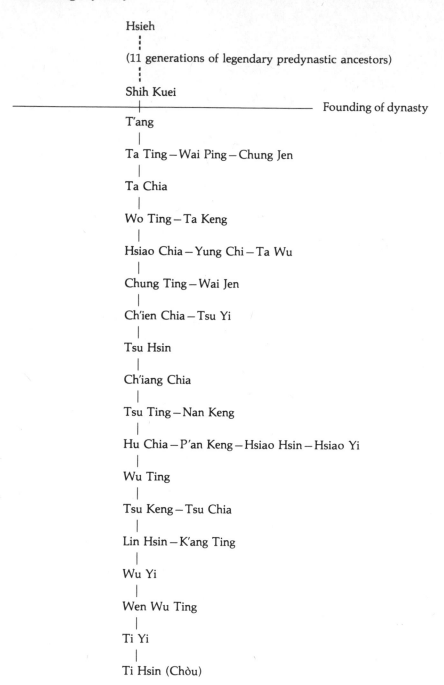

Hsieh
⋮
(11 generations of legendary predynastic ancestors)
⋮
Shih Kuei

——————————————————————— Founding of dynasty

T'ang
|
Ta Ting — Wai Ping — Chung Jen
|
Ta Chia
|
Wo Ting — Ta Keng
|
Hsiao Chia — Yung Chi — Ta Wu
|
Chung Ting — Wai Jen
|
Ch'ien Chia — Tsu Yi
|
Tsu Hsin
|
Ch'iang Chia
|
Tsu Ting — Nan Keng
|
Hu Chia — P'an Keng — Hsiao Hsin — Hsiao Yi
|
Wu Ting
|
Tsu Keng — Tsu Chia
|
Lin Hsin — K'ang Ting
|
Wu Yi
|
Wen Wu Ting
|
Ti Yi
|
Ti Hsin (Chòu)

——————————————————————— End of dynasty

The Chou Dynasty

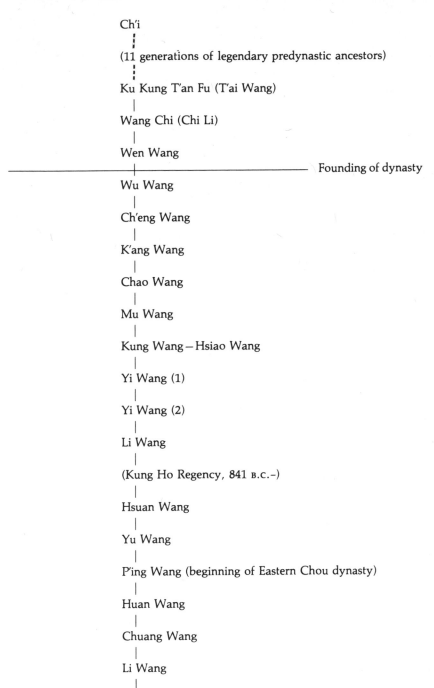

```
Ch'i
 ┊
(11 generations of legendary predynastic ancestors)
 ┊
Ku Kung T'an Fu (T'ai Wang)
 │
Wang Chi (Chi Li)
 │
Wen Wang
──────────────┼──────────────────────── Founding of dynasty
Wu Wang
 │
Ch'eng Wang
 │
K'ang Wang
 │
Chao Wang
 │
Mu Wang
 │
Kung Wang — Hsiao Wang
 │
Yi Wang (1)
 │
Yi Wang (2)
 │
Li Wang
 │
(Kung Ho Regency, 841 B.C.–)
 │
Hsuan Wang
 │
Yu Wang
 │
P'ing Wang (beginning of Eastern Chou dynasty)
 │
Huan Wang
 │
Chuang Wang
 │
Li Wang
 │
```

Huei Wang

Hsiang Wang

Ch'ing Wang

K'uang Wang — Ting Wang

Chien Wang

Ling Wang

Ching Wang (1)

Ching Wang (2)

Yuan Wang

Ting Wang

Ai Wang — Ssu Wang — K'ao Wang

Wei Lieh Wang

An Wang

Lieh Wang — Hsien Wang

Shen Ching Wang

Nan Wang

——————————————————————— End of dynasty, 256 B.C.

SOURCES OF ILLUSTRATIONS

1. Jung Keng, *Han Wu Liang Tz'u Hua Hsiang Lu* (Peking: K'ao-ku Hsüeh-she, 1936).

2. *China Pictorial* 7 (1976) and 11 (1974).

3. Photo taken by the author, with the permission of the Institute of Archaeology, Chinese Academy of Social Sciences.

4. Jung Keng, *Han Wu Liang Tz'u Hua Hsiang Lu* (Peking: K'ao-ku Hsüeh-she, 1936).

5. Lo Chen-yü, ed., *Ch'en Hsiao Erh-chia Huei Li Sao T'u* (Shanghai: Ch'an-yin-lu, 1924).

6. *Chung-kuo Li-tai Ming-jen Hua-hsiang Huei-pien* (Taipei: Wei-wen, 1977).

7. Photograph by Wulsin, from Mary Ellen Alonso and Joseph Fletcher, *China's Inner Asian Frontier* (Cambridge, Mass.: Peabody Museum, Harvard University, 1979), p. 23.

8. Nelson I. Wu, *Chinese and Indian Architecture* (New York: Braziller, 1963).

9. *Yung-lo Ta-tien*, vol. 9561, as quoted in *K'ao-ku Hsüeh-pao*, 1959 (2).

10. Photographs courtesy of the Chou Yuan Archaeology Team.

11. *Wen-wu*, 1981 (3).

12. Photo by the author, 1975.

13. *Tso Chuan*.

14. *Chia Ku Wen Pien* (Peking: Chung-hua, 1965).

15. Left: *Chung-kuo Ku Ch'ing-t'ung-ch'i Hsuan* (Peking: Wenwu, 1976). Right: courtesy of the Institute of Archaeology, Chinese Academy of Social Sciences.

16. *K'ao-ku*, 1972 (4).

17. Jen Ch'i-yun, *Chiao Miao Kung Shih K'ao*, as quoted in Ling Shun-sheng, "Chung-kuo tsu-miao chih ch'i-yüan," *Bulletin of the Institute of Ethnology, Academia Sinica* 7 (1959).

18. Jung Keng, *Han Wu Liang Tz'u Hua Hsiang Lu* (Peking: K'ao-ku Hsüeh-she, 1936).

19. Jung Keng, *Han Wu Liang Tz'u Hua Hsiang Lu* (Peking: K'ao-ku Hsüeh-she, 1936).

20. Lo Chen-yü, ed., *Ch'en Hsiao Erh-chia Huei Li Sao T'u* (Shanghai: Ch'an-yin-lu, 1924).

21. *Shan Hai Ching Ts'un*, 1895 edition.

22. Lo Chen-yü, *Yin-hsu Shu-ch'i Ching-hua* (Peking: Privately printed, 1914).

Sources of Illustrations

23. Bradley Smith and Wango Weng, *China: A History in Art* (New York: Harper & Row, 1973).

24. Li Chi, *Archaeologia Sinica*, n.s., various issues.

25. 1 and 2: Carl Hentze, *Objets rituels, croyances et dieux de la Chine antique et de l'Amérique* (Anvers: De Sikkel, 1936). 3: K. C. Chang, *The Archaeology of Ancient China* (New Haven: Yale University Press, 1977). 4: Douglas Fraser, "Early Chinese artistic influence in Melanesia?" in *Early Chinese Art and Its Possible Influence in the Pacific Basin*, ed. Noel Barnard (New York: Intercultural Arts Press, 1972). 5: *Yin-hsü Wu Hao Mu* (Peking: Wen-wu, 1980). 6: Li Chi, *The Beginnings of Chinese Civilization* (Seattle: University of Washington Press, 1957).

26. *Shan Hai Ching Ts'un*, 1895 edition.

27. W. Bogoras, *The Chukchee*, Memoirs of the American Museum of Natural History, vol. 11 (New York, 1909), pp. 317, 530.

28. *Shan Hai Ching Ts'un*, 1895 edition.

29. Li Chi, *Archaeologia Sinica*, n.s., 4 (1970).

30. Upper left from Sueji Umehara, *Studies of the Bronzes of the Warring-States Style* (Kyoto, 1936). The others are from K. C. Chang, *The Archaeology of Ancient China* (New Haven: Yale University Press, 1977).

31. *Chung-kuo Li-tai Ming-jen Hua-hsiang Huei-pien* (Taipei: Wei-wen, 1977).

32. *Wen-wu*, 1975 (8).

33. *K'ao-ku Hsüeh-pao*, 1981 (4).

34. *Shensi ch'u-t'u Shang Chou ch'ing-t'ung-ch'i*, vol. 2 (Peking: Wen-wu, 1980).

35. *Shensi ch'u-t'u Shang Chou ch'ing-t'ung-ch'i*, vol. 2 (Peking: Wen-wu, 1980).

36. Photo courtesy of the National Bureau of Cultural Relics, Peking.

37. *K'ao-ku Hsüeh-pao*, 1982 (1).

38. K. C. Chang, *The Archaeology of Ancient China* (New Haven: Yale University Press, 1977).

39. Noel Barnard and Satō Tamotsu, *Metallurgical Remains of Ancient China* (Tokyo: Nishiosha, 1975).

40. Shih Chang-ju, "Yin tai ti chu-t'ung kung-yi," *Bulletin of the Institute of History and Philology, Academia Sinica* 26 (1955).

41. *K'ao-ku Hsüeh-pao*, 1981 (4).

42. Top: Photograph on exhibit at the Lo-yang Archaeology Team, Institute of Archaeology, Chinese Academy of Social Sciences. Bottom: *Wen-wu*, 1976 (2).

43. Photo taken by Thomas Chase at Pan-p'o Museum, 1973.

44. *Hsi-an Pan-p'o* (Peking: Science Press, 1962).

45. Photographs courtesy of the Archaeology Program, Department of History, Peking University.

46. *Bulletin of the Museum of Far Eastern Antiquities* (Stockholm), vol. 15 (1945), vol. 19 (1947).

47. *Ta-wen-k'ou* (Peking: Wen-wu, 1974).

48. Hsü Hsü-sheng, *Chung-ku Ku-Shih ti Ch'uan-shuo Shih-tai* (Peking: Science Press, 1960).

49. Photo taken by the author in 1977, Lo-yang Archaeology Team, Institute of Archaeology, Chinese Academy of Social Sciences.

INDEX

Achilles, 97
Agricultural implements, 108, 109
Alcoholic drinks, 55
Alter ego: as motif in art, 74, 75
Ancestor: as factor in politics, 8
Ancestor cult, 37
Ancestral temple, 37, 40
Ancient China: chronology of, 2; defini-
  tion of, 1, 8
Anderson, Perry, 126
Animal: as alter ego, 74; in art, 56–78,
  116; bone of, as medium, 68; breath of,
  73; mythical, 57–59; in sacrifice, 65, 69,
  71; as shaman's helper, 65, 73; in Shang
  art, 70
Animal art, 107; iconography of, 61, 63,
  65; issues in, 61; meaning of, 61; pre-
  history of, 56, 63; as ritual parapher-
  nalia, 63, 64; as sheer design, 61
Animal design: symmetry of, 60, 75–78
Animal mask: prehistory of, 116
Animal motifs, 110
Animal offerings, 65
An-yang, 60, 72, 76; art of, 56, 57; and
  ores, 103. See also Yin-hsü
Archaeology: of politics, 108; as new tool
  of history, 5; as tool of prehistory, 4
Architecture: and politics, 110, 111
Art: 95, 107; and politics, 8, 56–80; and
  shamanism, 48. See also Animal art
Asiatic society, 126. See also Oriental
  society
Ax, 60, 62, 100

Aztecs, 74

Bear: in art, 57
Bird: in art, 56, 57
Boar: in art, 57
Bottle gourd: in ancestral myth, 15
Bronze: invention myth of, 96–97; uses
  of, 37, 108
Bronze Age, 5, 8, 101, 108, 110; agri-
  cultural implements in, 108
Bronze inscriptions, 89–90, 91, 92, 93
Bronze metallurgy, 101–106
Bronze vessels: ancient view of purposes
  of, 100; manufacture of, 101–106; and
  power politics, 106; as ritual parapher-
  nalia, 64, 101; as symbols, 97, 100;
  types of, 101, 102. See also Ritual
  vessels

Carpenter's tools, 108
Ch'ang sha, 79
Chariots, 37, 39, 107, 108, 110
Cheng-chou, 26, 98
Chi (clan), 12, 15, 20, 30, 42, 120
Ch'i (ritual vessels), 63
Ch'i (Mt.), 18, 20, 23
Ch'i (Chou Dynasty state in Shantung),
  30, 31
Ch'i (son of Yü), 10, 65, 95, 96, 131, 133.
  See also K'ai
Ch'i (founder of clan of Chou), 12
Chiang (clan), 12, 30
Chiang-chai, 83, 84, 112

137